SEEKING YOUR CENTER

SEEKING

YOUR CENTER

HOW TO ACHIEVE DEEPER FULFILLMENT
BY REDEFINING SUCCESS

TIM CRAIN
with JOEL WORLEY, PhD

© 2014 Tim Crain. All rights reserved. No part of this document may be reproduced or transmitted in any form or by any means, electronic or mechanical, including photocopying, recording, or by an information storage and retrieval system – except by a reviewer who may quote brief passages in a review to be printed in a magazine, newspaper, or on the Web – without permission in writing from the author.

Although the author and publisher have made every effort to ensure the accuracy and completeness of information contained in this book, we assume no responsibility for errors, inaccuracies, omissions, or any inconsistency herein. Any slights of people, places, or organizations are unintentional.

Cover Design by Brian Halley
Layout Design by Nikki Ward, Morrison Alley Design

First Printing 2014

ISBN 978-0-9960788-2-5

This book is dedicated to my wife, Amy, and our children. I love you and hope all of your dreams come true. But mostly, I hope you enjoy a centered life.

Table of Contents

Acknowledgments		i
Introduction		iii
Chapter 1	Seeking Your Center	1
Chapter 2	Why Do We Seek Center	13
Chapter 3	The Ingredients of a Centered Life	28
Chapter 4	Faith, Inner Peace, and Your Center	38
Chapter 5	The Five Tenets of Center	58
Chapter 6	Qualities of People Who Are Near Center	83
Chapter 7	Values, Priorities, and Internal Clarity	103
Chapter 8	Obstacles to Reaching Your Center	117
Chapter 9	Resources for Seeking Center	136
Chapter 10	Moving Toward Your Center	153
Conclusion	Living Near Your Center	167
Appendix 1	Searching for Center	181
Appendix 2	A Quick Overview of Seeking Your Center	190
About the Author		199

Acknowledgments

A book like this doesn't get written or finished without the help and guidance of a lot of different people. Although I started on this project many years ago, it has taken some key pieces of assistance and advice to actually bring it to life.

My special thanks go to Joel Worley, who served as an advisor and sounding board during the writing of this book and as my life mentor for the past two-plus decades leading up to it. I'll always be grateful for your wisdom and perspective.

Thank you to my executive coach, Anne Warfield, who convinced me to sit down and finish bringing *Seeking Your Center* to life.

To my colleagues, and especially those who took the time to comment on early drafts and concepts, I appreciate the personal stories and feedback you gave me. This book wouldn't have been as complete without your willingness to share your own thoughts and experiences.

All of my love and thanks to my mother for her consistent support and encouragement along life's way.

And finally, a word of thanks to my family, who has encouraged me while I tried to find a way to express something that's been building inside of me for so many years. You help me live a more centered life, and it's only because of you that I can try to share that gift with the rest of the world.

Introduction

There are probably dozens of reasons to write a book, but the one you're reading now was envisioned for a single, distinct purpose: *I want to help you change your life.* To be more specific, I want every day to feel more enjoyable, meaningful, and fulfilling.

Does that sound like a huge goal? Good. I decided early on in this process that "thinking big" was an important part of putting these ideas together. And even more importantly, I'm going to ask *you* to think big right along with me as we move through one chapter and section to the next. If you aren't willing to do that, then the time and money you spent to get this book into your hands (or on a screen in front of you) is going to be wasted.

To help you understand why, and how I came to this point, let me tell you a bit about myself and *Seeking Your Center*. Since I was a small boy, the people closest to me in my life have consistently remarked that I tend to think differently. I guess you could say I've always been interested in people, their goals, and the deeper meaning that so many of us struggle to find in the world around us.

For much of my life, this perspective was just another part of my personality. However, as my career progressed, and I began to glimpse the lives of ultra-successful men and women up close, I learned a truth that many of them can attest to: Traditional measures of success, and especially financial or material targets, almost *never* bring their recipients the long-term happiness they were hoping for.

Over time, I became incredibly curious about why this might be, even though I felt like the answers were already available on an intuitive level. It's no secret that material gain isn't a sure path to fulfillment – a piece of wisdom backed up by numerous books and psychological studies.

But, one question often goes unanswered: If so many of us are chasing our tails when it comes to contentment, fulfillment, and inner peace, why hasn't anyone developed a more reliable way to achieve them? And, why do so many supposed answers work for one person and not another? It turns out "happiness" and all that it entails is a very personal concept.

These kinds of questions led me on a search – one with internal and external dimensions. I wanted to know not just why people who are achieving their dreams aren't completely satisfied, but also how everyone else could avoid making the same mistakes. And, even more than that, I wanted to know how *all* of us could move toward a place in our lives where we feel engaged and fulfilled on a regular basis.

I knew tackling these kinds of ideas would be a big project, so I enlisted help from one of the smartest and wisest people I've ever known. That's why you'll see the name Joel Worley, PhD, on the cover of this book.

Joel has been through the joy and pain that come with living more than 70 years of a very full life. He's earned academic honors and taught thousands of college students in a number of different subjects. His real-world business experience spans decades and includes dozens of consulting projects. And, he's served as an advisor or counselor to countless friends, couples, and protégés – myself included.

As *Seeking Your Center* began to take shape, I also shared some of the concepts with friends and colleagues to see if I was on the right track. The response was literally overwhelming. A few got excited and either wanted to share their own experiences or hear about what I'd come up with so far. A handful actually got angry because the ideas I put forth brought up hard questions that they weren't willing to face themselves. And, more than a couple actually burst into tears, having years or decades of frustration pour out all at once.

While these reactions fell into wildly different categories, they all led me to the conclusion that *Seeking Your Center* touches a nerve. That is, lots of us feel like we aren't getting all from life that we could be, and there is a desperate need for an answer to a question that most people don't fully understand.

So, when I say I want to help you change your life, understand this isn't a ploy to get you to keep reading, but a recognition of the fact that we are going to be going a lot of places in this book. You might even be able to uncover ideas or feelings within yourself that you didn't know were there.

For that reason, this book isn't so much for *readers* as it is for *doers*. First you read, of course, but then you need to undertake the sometimes difficult process of self-assessment and exploration. You may have to begin a journal, wrestle with an idea repeatedly, or go back over a section multiple times. Each of these may try your patience, but they'll also bring the kinds of rewards you can't get from simply taking in a nice story on a set of pages.

Consciousness is a tricky thing. Although each of us is aware that our minds are moving at a rapid pace from one moment to the next, *we aren't always conscious of what we are conscious about*. In other words, it can be difficult to truly determine what's on our own minds. Add in the fact that all of us have lots of things going on at the unconscious level, as well, and it gets easy to see why finding your center isn't as simple as determining what your immediate career or personal goals are.

In my experience, the answer to this dilemma is to identify what really matters to you through the process of journaling.

I've used journaling and mind maps throughout my adult life and have always been amazed at the way putting your thoughts on paper can lead to breakthroughs of clarity and perspective. As an example, I can recall one

April afternoon I spent at a national business conference for my company. My business performance wasn't where I felt it should have been for the year and I was feeling a bit frustrated. Watching one colleague after another accept the awards and accolades I felt I should be receiving was just making my mood worse.

At some point during the day, a light bulb went on in my mind. I began to think it was possible I wasn't seeing things correctly, or at least with the right attitude. So, on a whim, I started making a list of all the *positive* things that had happened so far that year. Anything that mattered in my life or made me feel good was included.

After I got to the 130th item on my list, I went from being angry to just plain embarrassed. I was letting one bad day, and a few minor details, distract me from all the good I had in my life. It wasn't until I started actually putting my thoughts down on paper, though, that I was able to realize it.

That's what makes journaling so valuable. Even if it doesn't make you feel better about something, it can help you solidify your thinking and move you in the right direction.

As we move through the different topics and chapters in this book, you'll notice that I'm going to have a series of questions – titled *Searching for Center* – designed to help you start thinking about the most important ingredients to a fulfilling life. My hope is that you can use these as a starting point for your own journaling and uncover things about yourself that will lead you to a greater amount of happiness.

In fact, I encourage you to take a clean notebook and set it beside you as you go through this book. Make notes, draw pictures, cross out ideas or come back to them again and again. Do whatever it takes to help you find the understanding and clarity that led you to this point, because you aren't going to get the most from *Seeking Your Center* unless you do. I can show you the way, but you still have to take the steps yourself.

In case you move through the chapters without pausing to reflect, however, I've included copies of the questions again in the first appendix at the back of this book. You will also find a quick "recap" of *Seeking Your Center* with the most critical ideas and concepts put together in one place. As with the questions for self-discovery, these will be highlighted within the chapters as you go for extra emphasis.

I've taken these steps because I don't want this to be another book that you just read… I want it to be the catalyst that pushes you toward the kind of life you've been dreaming about living for a long time.

Now that you know a little bit about why I wrote this book, and what lies ahead, are you ready to start *Seeking Your Center?*

CHAPTER ONE

Seeking Your Center

"Why can't I find a way to be truly happy?"

If you've ever heard someone express that sentiment, or felt it yourself, you already know what a strange, unexpected idea it can be. Isn't happiness supposed to be a byproduct of doing more, or just being "better"? Our world is virtually built around the idea that finding material success – that is, climbing the ladder, earning more, and accumulating material assets – is the best and easiest way to earn more happiness, excitement, and fulfillment.

Why is it, then, that so many of us find ourselves yearning for something else, or something a little bit different... regardless of what might be happening in our lives? Why is it that even high-powered executives, well-known celebrities, and other high achievers suddenly lose interest in the targets they set for themselves and begin to wonder what it's all about? And even more importantly, what can you do to make sure you don't fall into the same trap?

That's what *Seeking Your Center* is all about. In this book, we are going to look at why traditional measurements of achievement often fall short, and why the differences between success, engagement, and fulfillment are more important than they've ever been in our modern world. We'll see why some people feel energized and content at the same time, while so many others have the sense that something is missing in their lives.

In short, we'll get to the root of the issue of what causes so many men and women to say things like:

"Why don't I feel happier with what I have?"

"I just wish I knew what comes next."

"I'm not really sure what I'm working for anymore, or if I even enjoy the path I'm on."

"I've done what I set out to do, so why don't I feel better about it?"

Each of these represents an element, or perhaps just a symptom, of a bigger overall struggle. And, even though the people whispering these things to their spouses and colleagues late at night tend to think that their problem or situation is unique, I know from firsthand experience that it isn't. In fact, not only are these thoughts common, but people have been wrestling with them for centuries.

From philosophers to business leaders, politicians to entertainers, history tells us that most people eventually come to a point where they start looking for a bigger meaning to their lives and careers, and for goals that extend beyond titles, salaries, and stock options. They effectively learn what any third-year psychology student can tell you: that material gains only take you so far toward happiness, and that the road to something better isn't one that can usually be charted on a resume. In other words, if we want to actually feel successful, we often have to change the definition of success we are working with in the first place.

My own road to this realization didn't go through a classroom. My whole life, I've had friends, colleagues, and mentors tell me that I have a different way of looking at the world. Looking back, I think a few of them might even have meant it as a compliment. What they sensed is that I was always looking for something beneath the surface, a meaning or focus that was obvious and hidden at the same time. That led me to start looking into the real nature of happiness, success, and inner peace.

By considering what things like "success" and "happiness" *really* mean to most of us, and the contradictory ways we try to find or create them, I started to notice patterns and traits among the people who have the highest levels of contentment. Those patterns turned into a system that was envisioned and developed over many years, refined and discussed several times over. What's left is a blueprint you can use to get more from your time on earth, regardless of where you are in your life right now.

What Finding Your Center Feels Like

When was the last time you felt completely exhilarated, locked in, and glad to be alive in a moment? When did you feel completely calm, in control, and at peace?

That sensation, which all of us have had at various points in our lives, is what I mean when it comes to "finding your center."

> It's about that mental and spiritual place where there isn't any fear or doubt, no worries or regrets, just the simple joy of doing whatever you're doing. It's not just having a sense of inner peace; it's *having the acknowledgment and awareness* that you do, and knowing that you can come back to that feeling again and again.

There are a lot of different ways to come to that sensation, and I'll get to a few of the most common in a moment. One of the best examples I've come across, however, has to do with reaching the summit of Mount Everest, the highest point on Earth.

As obvious as the analogy might be, it works extraordinarily well. If you talk to an experienced climber, they'll tell you each expedition is all about the journey, in that they truly love every step they take. And yet, reaching the summit isn't just another small move forward, or a minor accomplishment; instead, it's a revelation that sets their spine tingling. Looking out over the world for dozens of miles in any direction, feeling physically and mentally satisfied, they are often met with a moment that is *literally* beyond words. It's a state of both excitement and contentment, the sense that everything in their lives has led to that point.

As great an example as climbing offers, spending time on mountaintops isn't the only way to find center.

Some men and women seek it out in competitive sports, through charity work, or in hobbies like auto racing and private aviation. A lot of people would say they feel centered sitting across from their spouse sipping a glass of wine at a nice restaurant, being completely "chilled out" and at peace with the world. A few of us are lucky enough to feel it from time to time at work. And of course, lots of us stumble upon this feeling completely by accident, hoping and dreaming that we can recreate it again sometime in the future.

I can tell you that, in my own life, I am aware of feeling centered when I sit across from my beautiful wife over a candlelit dinner. I also feel satisfied and at peace when I see my children living their dreams. Watching their efforts and aspirations come to life is incredibly fulfilling. I get the same sensation from watching a team member being acknowledged for a job well done. At times like these, I appreciate being exactly where I am, and I'm living in the moment every bit as much as I would be rappelling or flying an open cockpit aircraft fifty feet above the sands of a beach.

So you see, you don't have to become an adventure athlete or adrenaline junkie just to find your center. It's a feeling you can get from spending an incredible day with a loved one, doing something significant for another person, or just fulfilling a wish you've always had inside of you. More often than not, the mountains we climb are mental and metaphorical, but the feeling of reaching the summit can be just as strong.

When we're actually in our center, top performance feels effortless, and we are getting the very best of ourselves. It's that combination of doing more, and doing it better, in the absence of stress and anxiety that makes finding center so important (not to mention a bit addictive). It's a sensation that most of us yearn for on an unconscious level even if we never take the time to actually think about why.

Before we get into the heart of this book, though, and the process of finding center, we should also make note of a few things that being centered *isn't*. For one thing, it's the complete opposite of the dull, lifeless sensation that leaves you feeling like you can't get out of bed in the morning, that life is overwhelming, or that you're just grinding out one day after the next. When you're at your center, you don't feel empty, struggling, or unfulfilled. You don't worry about where your life is going, or what you're really working toward. You are reflecting on the complete satisfaction you are experiencing at the moment.

In the same way, being centered doesn't necessarily mean that you are so "high on life" you don't notice daily annoyances or that you give up all of your worldly dreams and possessions to serve some charitable cause. Although those kinds of lifestyles might lead *some* people to feel more centered, most of us will find that we are happier staying away from the extremes.

> **In essence, finding center – whether it's for a moment or a lifetime – usually involves *exhilaration, purpose,* and *fulfillment.***

It's not an action, but a state of being. It lasts longest when all three elements are in place, but you can have wonderful experiences with just one or two ingredients, which is something we'll cover in the coming chapters.

SEARCHING FOR CENTER

✓ *When in the past have you felt completely centered?*

✓ *What ideas or activities have captivated you completely and stand out as being the most memorable in your mind?*

✓ *What does it take to feel your center?*

For now, just know that it's different from the feeling of simply being excited, because it moves you on a spiritual level as well as a physical one.

WAIT... IS THIS A BOOK ON SPIRITUALITY?

Let's take a moment with that ever-so-loaded word, *spiritual*. Obviously, "spiritual" can mean a lot of things to a lot of different people. What we can all agree upon, though, is that it's something that's a tricky subject for a lot of people. Because of that sensitivity, spirituality is something that's rarely ever discussed in corporate circles or public life. In fact, our society has made spirituality a subject that's practically taboo.

In my mind, that's unfortunate. As it turns out, a strong spiritual foundation can be a great source of strength, creativity, and perseverance, not to mention career achievement and real-world results. The key, however, is to find the spiritual center that works for you, whether or not it's defined by any religion or ideology. Your journey is *your* journey; it's ultimately going to be up to you to decide what you believe and can find faith in.

With that in mind, I'm going to ask you to stay a little bit open-minded through the following chapters. The only thing I'm going to require you to do is recognize the possibility, accepted and acknowledged over the centuries by virtually every major culture, that mankind might be a part of something bigger than each individual person. In other words, I want you to consider that your life, and your very existence, might amount to something more than a stack of possessions and genetics.

If you can stay with me on that train of thought, I think you'll find that considering something "spiritual" isn't as strange, or even nontraditional, as you might think. We'll explore how spirituality fits into the process of finding your center in coming chapters, but for the moment, just resolve to keep reading and trust me, regardless of whether you consider yourself to be a spiritual person or not.

How to Use This Book

As we move through the coming chapters and topics, I'm going to share what I've learned about finding your center and unlocking the key to a successful and fulfilling life. You should know from the beginning, however, that self-discovery is a big part of the process.

> **Unless you are willing to examine your own ideas, beliefs, and motivations, nothing I can write is going to be of value.**

To put things in a different perspective, every reader should understand that the concept of center is highly personal. *My* center isn't *your* center. For that reason, the answers that work for me might not make as much sense for you. Keep that in mind as you think about the exercises and examples that are provided. Just because something sounds good, or makes sense for a large number of people, doesn't make it the appropriate answer for you. Some ideas for finding your center are universal, but many aren't. I'll help you figure out which answers work for you.

The fact that you can't simply follow a set of straightforward instructions makes the job of finding your center more difficult, but also makes it more fun and interesting. After all, if it were as easy as moving through a checklist, everyone would do it and the results wouldn't be very meaningful. What we're shooting for here isn't a quick personality assessment, but a genuine sense of what's going to bring you joy and contentment through your career and personal life. That's an intensive process, but it's also well worth the effort.

And so, if you really want to get the most out of this book, it's incumbent upon you to expect to *do* as much as you *read*. Tempted as you might be to rush through the questions and activities you find, or skip over them altogether, I hope you can fight the urge. As the old saying goes, "You'll only be shortchanging yourself." There is a lot to be learned and gained by figuring out what truly motivates you at a core level and creating a personal roadmap to reach it; you just have to be willing to be honest with yourself and do what it takes to find the right answers.

Finding center isn't about filling in a questionnaire, and it's not the same as having an epiphany that you can never experience again. Instead, it's about building a life that's not only in line with your stated personal and professional goals, but also the parts of your personality that you might not think about on a conscious level all that often. When you're aware of what you're really working toward, feel good about it, and are excited to move forward, you'll be amazed at the difference it can make in all the parts of your life.

The First Step Is Always the Biggest

Are you ready to take the next step? Can you keep an open mind if the ideas ahead can lead you to more happiness, more fulfillment, and even more success?

I hope so. Over the years, I've gotten the chance to present these ideas and show how they have worked for me and in the lives of some of the most successful and satisfied men and women I know. It is my wholehearted belief that anyone can take the insight and advice in the following chapters, make them their own, and use them to great effect.

I want the next success story to be yours, so let's begin our journey toward center together...

CHAPTER TWO

Why Do We Seek Center?

To me, the process of searching for excitement, meaning, and contentment in our lives – what I call seeking center – is almost instinctual. It cuts across cultures and generations so cleanly and completely that I consider it to be an integral part of the human condition. On one level or another, I believe we all want to be something more, or part of something bigger.

But, as I've already mentioned, that doesn't make the process of finding that meaning and truth simple or straightforward, and the answers can vary from one person to the next. And so, finding your center can be difficult. It's no wonder that so many people eventually give up, deciding that what they're feeling will pass, or what they're looking for can't be found in this life.

I'm not going to tell you I have a way to make finding your center easy, because for most people it isn't. But I'm going to remind you that it's *possible*. And even more importantly, that it's necessary and helpful. That's because, for all the nonspecific emotional aches and pains that come from being *off* your center, there are just as many real and tangible reasons to take up the journey.

The Personal Benefits of Finding Center

The most profound benefit to discovering where your center lies is that it removes an ache and gives the sense of finding a missing piece. It's like scratching an itch that you could never reach in the past. That's not a small thing, especially as you go through more and more of your life and discover that nothing else can take the place of true fulfillment.

As I mentioned in the introduction, I began sharing some of these concepts with friends and coworkers as the chapters of this book came together. That provoked a lot of intense responses, but one in particular stands out in my mind. One night a colleague of mine, someone who had reached "success" many times over by any traditional measuring stick, listened to me talk about what the book would cover. Although I only spoke for a few minutes, his eyes seemed to wander as his mind drifted farther and farther away. Eventually, he only nodded absently at me to show he was still listening.

When I had finished, he related to me that – despite all the awards, accolades, and possessions that had come his way – he had felt like he had a large hole in his life that he was personally unable to fill. There was a yearning, but he couldn't identify what he was actually yearning *for*. For years and years, the question nagged at him, but he was never able to make sense of it.

In my experience, this isn't unusual. A lot of people, even those who have undergone intense self-discovery in the past, know that they have gaps in their lives but struggle to identify them. If you count yourself within that category, the process outlined in this book can help you build a roadmap toward finding what you're really looking for. And of course, those realizations are going to "spill over" into other parts of your life.

That's not just a nice theory, but a way of dealing with change that has saved me time and time again. I can remember a period in my life when my family was growing and my company was restructuring. My wife and I were being uprooted to a new community hundreds of miles away, and I was having to adapt to new responsibilities all at the same time. Things seemed so overwhelming that I was sleepless and paralyzed with doubt and uncertainty. My world seemed to be spinning out of control, and all of my hopes and plans were being swept along with it.

By focusing on my personal center, I was able to separate major priorities from minor setbacks. I got back in touch with what actually mattered to me and was able to shut out much of the "noise" that was really just part of an adjustment period. My sense of calm returned, and in time I was on even stronger footing than before. Without a roadmap back to my center, though, I could easily have found myself adrift and confused, as so many people eventually do when they experience upheaval in their lives.

> **People who are at or near their center exude a calm and confidence that seems impossible to those who don't have it.**

They are able to see situations more clearly, and react to day-to-day problems in a way that's in line with the kind of life they are trying to build, rather than randomly bouncing from one mood or impression to the next.

One side effect of that increased calm and decreased pressure is that creative instincts become more powerful. That doesn't necessarily mean you'll get to work on a stunning novel or a masterpiece painting, but it *does* mean that you'll probably find you can form connections and generate inspiration in the parts of your life that are most important to you.

Another side effect is that men and women who are at center often find themselves feeling and being healthier. It has long been known that stress can be as damaging to your body as any disease over the course of time. Because finding your center necessarily decreases the amount of tension you feel, and takes away a lot of your apprehension and worries for the future, it is naturally calming and relaxing. It might not cure illnesses and injuries, but it can potentially help prevent chronic health problems while giving you more energy and vitality than you've felt in a long time. When you have renewed purpose and direction, you just feel better.

For most people, these benefits alone would be enough to make finding your center worth the process of reflection and self-discovery. But, we should also consider the other side of the coin, and revisit some of the problems that come when you feel like you're away from your center.

Instead of calm and peace, you have irritability and a nagging suspicion that you aren't doing the right things at the right time. You might feel like your potential is going unfulfilled, or find yourself being overly aggravated by small problems and agitations. In other words, the "little-picture" stuff tends to crowd out the wider view of where you're headed in your life. You may not sleep well or feel like you can relax; instead of tension melting away, it gets a little bit stronger and more burdensome each day.

Even worse, the farther you get from your center, the more severe these problems tend to become. In some cases, people will turn to addictive behaviors and substances just to close off the voices in their minds. Even though they can't describe exactly what it is that's bothering them, they'll go to great lengths to tune out the whispers telling them that they aren't headed in the right direction.

That isn't to say that you should try to put your life and career on a different path simply because you want to avoid pain, but rather a simple recognition that finding your center is a matter of psychological, emotional, and spiritual balance. And as most of us already know, balance is two sides of the same coin – everything in your life is easier when you feel aligned, and anything you try to do is that much harder when you don't.

It's also important to remember that the benefits of being centered aren't always completely personal. They also extend to our careers, our families, and every other group we happen to touch or interact with.

What Finding Center Does for Your Career

Although we have thus far referred to personal and professional lives separately, the reality is that the separation isn't as clear-cut as most of us think it is. Our working lives and family lives, for instance, frequently collide and overlap. It's the same way when we are thinking about the concept of finding center.

> **Rarely do people find complete professional fulfillment when their personal lives are in tatters, or vice versa.**

This runs a bit contrary to popular thinking. The idea of the overworked, overstressed man or woman who excels in the office at the expense of a social life is a common cliché on television and in movies. And yet, if you study the highest achievers in almost any field, you'll find that the vast majority have the support of friends and family behind them, and usually have interests and accolades that extend far beyond their professional duties.

Besides, common sense tells us that a person who is calm, focused, and energetic is going to be a better leader or professional than someone who isn't. Likewise, the kind of person who can remain steady in the face of pressure and feel good about where they're headed in their career is probably going to enjoy a happier home life, as well.

And so, even though this isn't a book that's explicitly about goal setting, leadership, or career planning, I absolutely think the process you'll go through in *Seeking Your Center* could be the best thing that ever happens in your working life. You'll come out the other side a stronger person, and one who knows how to separate what's truly important from all the "noise" surrounding them. That kind of vision and strength can only help you with any career move or volunteer project you engage in for the rest of your life.

What I'm really hoping you'll get from this book isn't just a set of tips, or even a new perspective.

> **What I want you to walk away with is a permanent mental re-framing that can help guide you through the rest of your life.**

I'm talking about a different way of thinking and being, one that leads to greater insight about yourself and a deeper level of fulfillment than you can find without taking this journey.

People who are at or near their center have an attractive quality about them. That makes extroverts natural leaders, and introverts more effective communicators, because they are able to draw upon an energy and enthusiasm that others don't have. This isn't some sort of trick or gimmick; they are focused and excited because they care, and they're able to use those qualities to get others to pitch in and work for common goals.

If you doubt the power of that benefit, contrast that dynamic against the leaders or individuals you've known in your life who try to create a false sense of teamwork, shared goals, and motivation. When they try to pull others toward objectives that aren't meaningful, or targets that don't really matter (or that they themselves don't personally believe in), it rings false and others tend to not respond. In the same way that those who are at or near their center seem to have magnetic personalities, people who aren't near their centers can often unconsciously push others away, both personally and professionally.

Finding your center also helps you develop perseverance. After all, once you know absolutely that your life and career are moving in directions you want to see them take, there are very few setbacks that seem important enough to dwell on. That doesn't stop challenges from creeping into your life, of course, but it equips you to see them differently, and deal with them differently, than you might have in the past. You become a greater source of strength, both for yourself and others.

And finally, finding your center could make you more effective with your time for the same reasons. When you're on a mission to get something done, and that something matters to you very much, you aren't as apt to let minor distractions waste your day. You just have more important things to do.

The bottom line is that finding your center isn't necessarily about your career, or at least it's *bigger* than developing a professional skill. But being a stronger, more focused, and more efficient person is always going to be a good thing, whether you're at work or enjoying the other parts of your life.

How Finding Your Center Redefines Your Relationships with Others

In the same way that becoming more centered, energetic, and focused is going to naturally have an impact on your professional life, know that it can't help but spill over into your relationships with others, too. As you become a better version of yourself, the way others are going to think about you is going to be different than it was in the past. For the most part, that's a great thing.

After all, we are all naturally drawn to those who have passion and excitement in their lives. It's also likely that carrying lower stress, being more confident, and having fewer complaints about everyday nuisances is going to make you an easier person to be around. We can all use more happy and fulfilled people in our lives, so you might discover that some of your friends and contacts that didn't seem to be available in the past have time for you now.

On the other hand, there may be some in your life who are actually pushed away by your desire to find meaning and purpose. Believe it or not, this is something that experts will tell you is common to virtually any form of self-improvement. Strange as it might be, there are a lot of people who feel threatened by others taking steps they're afraid to take, or looking for the answers that they themselves are too scared to face.

There are a lot of people in this world who hold on to their own misery and disappointment as if it were an integral part of their personality. Start to strip yours away, and they are reminded that they haven't chosen to do the same.

Those aren't going to be the people you most need to be around, anyway. And it probably won't take you very long to replace them in your life. One of the big benefits of moving closer to your center is that you start to be drawn to other people who are close to their centers, as well. In that way, this sort of internal success is almost like a networking edge – focused, motivated people like to know and associate with one another.

By now you've probably started to wonder what kinds of things you might be able to accomplish if you had your mind firmly set in a positive direction. Now, with those possibilities firmly in mind, imagine what you might be able to get done with five or ten *other* focused people on your side. The results could literally be transformative, and that's something we're going to explore next…

Be the Change

To paraphrase Gandhi, "We should all strive to represent the kinds of changes we want to see in the world, to actively work to make them happen, instead of just wishing for them." At the risk of sounding a bit grandiose, imagine what kinds of things we can accomplish together if we were all putting the very best versions of ourselves forward, working on ideas that kept us truly engaged.

If that were normal, or at least not unusual, humanity would be transformed at virtually every level. Families would interact in a more personal, honest way, and we'd form stronger bonds with one another. Friendships could endure almost anything, and those we spend our time with would feel like the family we love. Good companies could grow and thrive, with leaders springing up in every department and whole teams committed to success. Even governments could flourish, with committed men and women making strong choices for the futures of their constituents, rather than pandering for votes.

Instead, though, we live in an age where things seem almost the opposite. Lots of people struggle to make a real connection with one another, partly because they feel agitated, stressed out, and directionless. Friends are often just trumped-up acquaintances, and the majority of the people we work with seem to approach their jobs with a focus on what they can get from employment, rather than what they can put into it. Teams work like collections of individuals, and governments barely work at all.

By choosing to actively find your passion and live your life in a way that's consistent with your mental and spiritual goals, you can create an effect that actually rubs off on those around you. Things like honesty and enthusiasm are contagious. The more of them you take into yourself and put out in the world, the better the world around you gets.

That's not to say that everyone is going to magically change overnight, or that the difficult people you have to deal with are going to stop thinking of themselves first. But, if enough of us would be committed to putting ourselves into balance and finding our center, we'd be a lot better prepared to show a little empathy and compassion to others. And in the end, who knows where that could lead?

The world doesn't get better, more helpful, or more considerate all on its own. If we want to be surrounded by others who care, and leave a healthier and happier planet for our kids and grandkids, then moving past traditional answers and trying to find our own sense of purpose isn't a bad first step.

Positive Feedback Cycles

If you read between the lines, you'll notice that what we are really talking about are positive feedback cycles. In case you aren't familiar with the term, it's where one good thing springs a lot of other good things into action, creating an avalanche or tipping point of positive benefits.

For an easy example of how this happens, consider someone who switches from an unhealthy lifestyle to a healthy one. When a person is in poor physical shape, a diet of junk food, a lack of exercise, and too much body weight can leave them feeling tired, depressed, and rundown. The natural result of that is that they crave more junk food, get even less active, and start to suffer more health problems. The cycle goes on and on until things are so far out of whack that the process seems irreversible.

But let's say that they decide to make a change. At first, they only get a bit of light exercise, but they also start to eat more healthful foods. Before long, they are losing weight, getting more restful sleep, and feeling more energized. What happens as a result? You already know – those improvements lead to more enthusiasm, more activity, and even better eating. The same kind of cycle that left them depressed and out of shape swings in the other direction and toward a healthier, happier future.

For most people, finding center is the same way. For those who are at or close to their center, life and work are energizing, filled with rich experiences and fulfilling relationships. Things are moving steadily in the right direction, and it's easy for them to feel motivated and content all at the same time. They also recognize that their feelings and perspectives have changed, which in turn lets them enjoy every experience more fully.

When someone is far from their center, though, it's easy for things to spiral in the other direction. Because they have the persistent feeling that something is missing from their lives, they try to cover the hole with other things. Perhaps they eat or drink more than they should, or seek out the wrong kinds of relationships. Or, they use work to stay busy and take their minds off the fact that their lives aren't as fulfilling as they'd like them to be. That kind of logic doesn't do any good in the long run, so the negative feedback cycle gets worse and worse, until it seems like there aren't any other choices.

> **The great thing is that as long as you're breathing, it's never too late to start moving toward your center**.

You always have choices, and what you do or learn can help point you in the right direction regardless of where you've been in the past. It never matters where you start in life, only where you finish.

In the next few chapters, we'll look at how you actually find your center and live in a way that keeps you there. It might not be as easy as we would like, but the rewards are even greater than most of us would ever hope for.

CHAPTER THREE

The Ingredients of a Centered Life

If your center is something you can actually find, rather than stumble into accidentally, then what can you do to reach it? What ingredients or elements have to be in place for you to feel content, energized, and fulfilled?

In this chapter, we're going to take a look at the cornerstones of the centered life. We'll be exploring all of them in greater detail in the coming sections, but I want to take a moment to introduce each of them briefly so you'll know what you're in store for, and so you can begin to get a sense of how the different elements work together with one another.

It's important to understand that your center doesn't come from one single area of your life. You can't buy your center or be promoted into it, and neither can you meet the right partner and have them pull you all the way to your center. You can't even get there through exercising love, charity, or a great amount of spiritual awareness, if the other parts of your life aren't in alignment.

This is a classic misunderstanding that lots of people have, and one that leads to mistakes of single-mindedness. There are a lot of really great things you can do with your time, and a lot of directions that you'll find incredibly fulfilling, but if you don't understand how the different pieces work together in the greater puzzle, you're going to struggle to feel centered on a consistent basis.

Let's take a quick look at the various ingredients of a centered, successful life.

Awareness of Your Center

It only makes sense that, in order to feel centered and fulfilled, you have to be aware of what it takes to make that happen. Obviously, that's something you're addressing right now by reading this book, but it's important to point out because awareness and knowledge aren't the same thing. In other words, when you put your attention and focus on living a life that makes you feel engaged, good things start to happen. And conversely, when you take your attention and awareness away from your center, you naturally tend to drift from it, as well.

> **As you'll discover again and again, your center isn't a stationary target, but a state of being that's always moving.**

It's altered by your living circumstances in an ongoing way, not to mention your changing values and priorities. For that reason, having an awareness of your center – and adapting your approach to the principles in this book to respond to these changes – is important if you're going to experience your center more frequently.

Faith and Spirituality

You don't have to subscribe to any particular religious belief to reach your center, but you do need to trust in something outside of yourself. You have to have a certain level of faith that there is a higher power at work in the universe, and a kind of plan or purpose that you can put your trust in.

The reason that faith and spirituality matter so much to the process of seeking your center is because they give you a sense of perspective, and an outside support system, that you can turn to time and time again. And, just as importantly, they can stop your thoughts from drifting inward so that you don't become obsessed with yourself and your own problems or challenges.

You'll notice here that the faith and spirituality we are talking about have to do with belief and acceptance, rather than rituals and practices. We'll look at this in more depth very soon, but it's important to know at this point that spirituality is incredibly important to reaching your center. Believing in any particular religious faith, however, is not necessarily a prerequisite.

Removing Obstacles

Because we all inherently want to live at or near our center, but few of us actually do, it stands to reason that there are several different prominent obstacles that lie in our way. By exploring and understanding them, we can clear the hurdles that stop us from living the kinds of lives we really want.

Some of the obstacles to reaching your center are physical while others are mental or emotional. Many of them may be so deeply ingrained that we never consciously think of them at all. That doesn't mean they aren't there, though, or that ignoring them will cause them to go away.

For most people, part of the process of seeking center involves letting go of certain past notions, ideas, or expectations. They have to shrug off the spiritual and emotional "dead weight" that holds them back. This can be difficult and tiring, but it's certainly not impossible, and it's always worth the effort.

Personal Values and Priorities

Each of us has goals, principles, and ideas that are critical to happiness and fulfillment in our own lives. However, those values and motivations aren't always known, even to ourselves, and in fact can be in direct conflict with one another.

One of the greatest sources of angst and frustration is living the kind of life that doesn't allow you to fully express or satisfy one of your underlying values and motivations. Understanding what they are is the first step, and then building a life that incorporates all of them – even the ones that might seem trivial and unimportant in the greater scheme of things – is the next.

By taking the time to properly think about what actually matters to us personally and then making a plan to live in accordance with our values and priorities, we don't just feel happier, but we also remove heavy burdens from ourselves that could otherwise stop us from reaching our centers.

The Tenets of Center

While some values and priorities are personal, five tenets of center – the parts of our lives that absolutely have to be in order for us to feel calm, content, and energized – are universal across cultures and generations.

We'll look at these more closely, of course, but they involve spiritual awareness, a strong inner circle, financial harmony, the purpose of self, and a lifestyle that's in alignment with the values and priorities we discussed a moment ago. You can think of these as different legs of a stool, each one supporting us on a day-to-day basis. When all are strong, we feel rooted and grounded. We can find our centers under those conditions.

When one or more of these tenets *aren't* in balance, on the other hand, achieving peace of mind is virtually impossible. In the coming chapter, I'm going to show you how to understand these five tenets and use them to pull yourself toward your center.

Resources

Each of us needs certain people in our lives in order to grow and thrive. If you doubt this, consider the way prison inmates react to solitary confinement, considered to be one of the harshest punishments available. Even in that kind of antisocial atmosphere, grown men and women fear being left alone almost more than they do anything else.

Whether we are conscious of it or not, we also need others to find and live at our centers, although not just anyone will do. To actually grow, feel supported, and challenge ourselves, we need someone who comforts us, professional counselors who can provide outside perspective, mentors who can lead the way, and spiritual advisors who keep us grounded in our faith.

As part of the process of seeking center, you'll learn why each of these is so important, and how to integrate these people and relationships into your life.

All Ingredients Work Together

As we explore the key concepts and ingredients of your center more thoroughly, you'll see that they all have to work together to create the intended effect. Without each of the tenets in place, for example, you can't feel mentally at ease, or enjoy a sense of energized creativity. If you lack in faith and spirituality, you'll inevitably end up dwelling on daily troubles because you don't have the right perspective. With no mentors to help you understand the path you're on, your sense of purpose and direction will falter.

I could go on and on, but what I want to instill in you is a sense that you can't pick and choose which parts of your life you're going to make the most of if you are truly going to find your center. You can get closer by working on one or two, perhaps, but you can't ever find peace and contentment unless you're willing to follow all the steps that are necessary.

Does This Process for Seeking Center Really Work?

At this point in the book, you might be excited and a little bit skeptical at the same time. Finding out how to live near your center certainly *sounds* great, but is it something that's actually achievable?

I can tell you from personal experience that it absolutely is. But, as I've pointed out already – and will continue to do throughout the following chapters – that centered feeling isn't something I can give to you. I can show you the way, but you have to go out and take it.

In that way, this book isn't a step-by-step guide to happiness, contentment, and inner peace. Instead, it's more like a metal detector. I can show you how to start looking for your happiness, what the major steps and components are, and how you can identify the pieces that might be missing in your life. But it's up to you to follow the internal signals you receive to keep getting closer and closer until you zero in on exactly what you're looking for. Some parts of being centered are universal to all humans; others are unique to you.

What's more, the mental and spiritual challenges we face are largely individual, as well. And so, even though every person reading this book should be moving more or less in the same direction, the path they have to take to reach it could vary quite a bit.

That means what's required of you isn't just to follow the steps and activities outlined, but also to pursue them with the right spirit and attitude. One thing that Joel and I have noticed in our experiences is that everyone comes through life damaged in some ways. We all have scars, both emotional and physical, that have helped us to become the people we are, for better or worse.

Often, one of the ways that we deal with these mental and emotional scars is to embrace skepticism. To a certain degree, that can be healthy.

> **You definitely don't want to be the kind of person that will fall for anything. Neither, though, do you want to be the sort of person who won't *believe* in anything, either.**

Once you take on that mindset, finding any kind of lasting happiness and contentment just isn't possible, because you aren't open to change and improvement in your life.

We all know people who are perpetually miserable. In fact, the only thing that seems to make them remotely happy is reminding themselves and others how unhappy they actually are. While this might be understandable from a coping perspective, it's not the way to find inner peace.

With that in mind, I want to make it clear that if you are the kind of person who disbelieves everything, or who doesn't truly believe that life can get any better than it is right now, you're going to struggle and ultimately fail with the concepts in this book. That isn't because they don't work, but because you will have dismissed them out of hand before giving them a fair shot.

If that's the case, you can do one of two things. First, you can put this book away on a shelf, or delete it from your tablet. It's okay, I won't take it personally. Or, you can decide to put your skepticism aside – even if it's just for a few hours – and imagine what might be possible if you approach these chapters' exercises with a different frame of mind. Could it be that you might be able to live your life in a different, more fulfilling way? What would you really have to risk to find out?

Finding your center is a process that is both self-defined and self-defining. By that I mean much is dependent on your own personality and experiences, but also that going through it tends to solidify your dreams and beliefs. It's a good way to answer that question, "Who am I, *really*?"

Seeking Your Center works, but you have to make it work by following along and putting your heart and soul into self-discovery. With this little bit of understanding in place, it's time to start closing in on your personal center.

CHAPTER FOUR

Faith, Inner Peace, and Your Center

At this point, I hope you're convinced that finding your center is worth the journey, and that the advice you find in this book is going to help you get there. Because, for the next few chapters, we're going to go a little bit deeper.

As I've already explained, the process of finding your center has a little to do with knowing what you're looking for, and a *lot* to do with the level of self-exploration and open-mindedness you're willing to show. That's something to keep in mind as we look more closely into the topics of spirituality, inner peace, and faith.

For some of you, and especially those who have strong religious beliefs, these might be words you use every day;

for others, they might seem like a giant "red flag" that you have stumbled into the wrong part of the wrong book. I understand. Still, I'm going to ask you to stick with me just a little bit longer. All I need for you to do, in order to help you find your center, is recognize that there can be something out there that exists beyond your own mind.

You'll notice that I didn't tell you that you have to believe in God, or take up any kind of particular religious viewpoint. What I'm really looking for here is an acknowledgment of a "higher power" in the same sense that twelve-step groups use the concept.

As part of the addiction recovery process, those who are looking to break destructive patterns that they've held on to in the past (and coincidentally, move closer to their centers) are asked to simply accept that there could be *something* bigger than all of us at work in our lives. It doesn't matter whether they consider that to be something secular, like the power of the universe, just that they stay open to its existence.

When we do that, we give ourselves something to stay grounded to that's bigger and more powerful than our own emotions or perceptions. It's a matter of perspective. When you realize that not everything is about you, you also discover that there are ideas you can tap into that are more powerful than your own thinking. That's where spirituality comes into play.

Ultimately, it's going to be up to you to decide how spiritual you are, and how much of a role your spiritual side is going to play in your life. Just know that if you ignore this part of yourself, you're ultimately going to regret it and it's going to be very hard to find your center.

This realization can be a hard pill to swallow for some people, but it doesn't have to be. If you struggle with religion (and in particular, a certain kind of *organized* religion), don't let that hold you back from exploring and expressing your spiritual side. Although the two often go together, they don't necessarily have to. You can definitely have spirituality without religion; and sadly enough, we've seen again and again that you can certainly have religion without spirituality.

Even people who aren't at all religious find that they have a spiritual yearning that needs to be met. In fact, we often find that men and women will go to great lengths to connect with something larger than themselves if that basic human necessity has been taken from them.

Because this is such a powerful and important concept, let's take a moment to look at a couple of quick examples...

THE NEED FOR A SPIRITUAL CONNECTION

Most of us don't have to go very far to find an example of someone who wants to be more in touch with their spiritual side. If we haven't been there ourselves, we probably know friends or relatives who have gone to great lengths to find a bigger, deeper meaning in their lives.

At the moment, though, I want to focus on a specific historical example, if only because I think it perfectly illustrates the point I'm trying to make.

World War I saw some of the most bitter, desperate fighting mankind has ever known. Buried in cold, dark, and diseased trenches across Europe, young men dug themselves in for weeks and months at a time, fearing to even move or catch a glimpse of the sky above, in case an enemy should be ready to end their lives. In addition to the obvious horrors of war that we still have with us today, the soldiers faced chemical attacks, bayonet rushes, and even starvation on a regular basis.

It would be hard to even imagine a worse situation for the human spirit. And yet, when it came down to it, it was proven again that we are all relatively alike in the ways that matter most, and there is a universal recognition of the human condition that spans borders and generations.

This was demonstrated perfectly in 1914 when, in the midst of heavy fighting, soldiers on both sides spontaneously decided that a truce should be observed for Christmas. Although the fighting stopped in many different places, the truce was completely unofficial and uncoordinated by governments and commanders. The young men who were completely intent on killing each other prior to the break in hostilities simply decided to stop for a few days. Amazingly enough, gifts were even exchanged between the different armies.

What does the Christmas truce of 1914 have to do with spirituality? In a word, *everything*. If you're following my definition of spirituality, which doesn't have anything to do with religion but everything to do with a recognition that we are all in this together (regardless of what you think "this" actually is), it's a great illustration of the human spirit. What's more, it's far from unique. We have seen again and again throughout history that people are willing to set aside their differences in times of crisis and celebration.

In fact, pay attention the next time you hear about an earthquake, tsunami, or other tragedy on TV. You'll learn that our natural impulse is to pitch in and see how we can help, even if there isn't anything to be gained or it's contrary to our normal everyday motivations.

The same impulse that makes us want to volunteer at a soup kitchen or help out children in need is the one that drives us to look for meaning and peace when those things are hard to find. When we aren't in some kind of connection with our spiritual selves, we feel a hole that can't be filled any other way. And more to the point, if we aren't nurturing our spiritual selves, we can't reach our center and find the inner peace we crave.

A Different Way to Think About Your Spiritual Life

To get at the importance of your spiritual center from another direction, consider the romantic relationships you have in your life.

It's easy to be attracted to someone, and you can in fact be physically attracted to lots of different people during the course of your dating years. If you get a chance to date several of them, as most of us do, you quickly learn that *attraction* is quite a bit different than *connection*. One can be quick, fleeting, and even one-sided, while the other tends to be lasting and enduring. In fact, as strong as an attraction can be, you'll have a much happier life if you find a partner with an enduring emotional connection that is even greater than the physical appeal.

Or, to put things more simply and traditionally, great relationships are built upon real love, not just physical desire.

In my mind, those connections we are talking about – the ones that most of us think of as emotional – are actually somewhat spiritual in nature. In the same way that the human condition is universal, the act of truly coming together as a couple is so much more than a chemical reaction.

Most of us have known a married couple that has been together for decades on end. They may or may not agree on everything, but you can see the love that exists between them in every moment and interaction. The bond they have is certainly more than physical, and can't even really be described as mental or emotional. In my mind, that's a truly *spiritual* connection existing between two different people.

If you can take that perspective, then you can understand why you need to have a spiritual element to your life. There can be lots of aspects to your career, relationships, and habits that you like, or even have a kind of "lust" after, but you're only going to be fulfilled if you feel in love with the life you have and have an appreciation of the direction you're moving in. That's the difference between excitement and contentment, and what separates an adrenaline rush from deep fulfillment.

To better understand this analogy, though, there are two things you have to keep in mind. The first is that not everyone you feel connected with has to represent a romantic interest for you. You might have a friend, mentor, or relative that you feel very close to despite the complete lack of a physical attraction. In the same way, there can be parts of your ideal, centered life that you can love even though they aren't necessarily the ones that get your pulse racing.

The other thing you have to remember is that all enduring relationships, even the ones where you have a wonderful connection, require *work*. Although they might begin in an instant, they require an effort to keep up, and usually grow the most during periods that seem to test and strain. The most difficult circumstances will ultimately make the best relationships stronger.

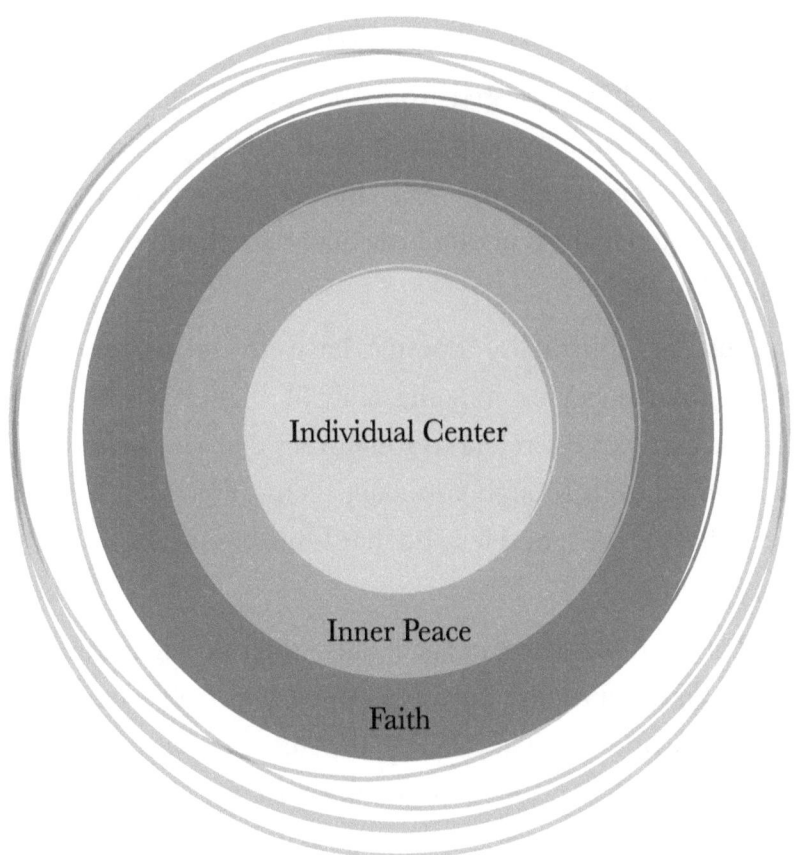

The same can absolutely be said of your quest to find center and live a life that you're in love with. Your goals and ambitions are going to change over time, and not everything you do to become centered is going to make you feel happy and excited in the moment. In fact, there might be periods where you wish you could do the easy thing and go in another direction away from your center. When that happens, remember that connection is more important than attraction, and fulfillment goes so much deeper than momentary interest and excitement.

From Spirituality to Faith

As you might've guessed from the title of this chapter, I consider spirituality and faith to be deeply intertwined topics. Before I tell you why, though, let's take a quick moment to clear up another misunderstood and somewhat loaded word.

Just as spirituality doesn't have to mean anything more than believing in some kind of higher power, faith in this context just refers to something that you believe (or believe in) even though you can't see it. That's not such a complicated idea, and it's one that I think you can probably agree with.

For example, you can't pull out a ruler and measure the love your parents have for you, or prove with 100% certainty that the world won't end before the sun rises tomorrow, but you have faith in both of those things. In fact, if you stop to think about it, you actually have faith in dozens and dozens of different things, like the value of the money in your bank account, or our collective ability to understand each other when we speak the same language.

In a bigger sense, faith is extraordinarily important because it allows us to experience peace of mind when it comes to our actions, decisions, and life direction.

> **Spirituality is accepting that there is something bigger to the universe, and faith is putting a little bit of our trust into that something.**

That's all there is to it. It's a small step, but one you *have* to take if you're going to reach your center. That's because faith is integral to the process, and for a few different reasons.

Why You Need Faith to Find Center

Does some kind of faith have to be tied to the search for balance, contentment, and fulfillment? I absolutely believe it does.

Here is why: Without any kind of faith in a higher power, or sense that there is anything more to the universe than what we see directly in front of us, we are left with the feeling that we can only trust and believe in ourselves. Even though a certain level of self-confidence can be extremely beneficial to your life, too much self-importance holds you back. It stops you from seeing the bigger picture and limits your perspective.

Personal achievements can be satisfying in the short term, but ultimately tend to be less gratifying. If you doubt this, spend a few hours with someone who has an active charitable life. They'll be the first to tell you that the time they spend on their causes gives them great personal pleasure. It might not be as fun or exciting as taking an exotic vacation, for example, or driving a very expensive car, but it leaves them with a sense of having changed lives, or the world as a whole, for the better.

This is even true for people who have some of the finer things in life. Acting charitably, and fulfilling that side of your personality, doesn't have to preclude material success. Remember that the point of this book isn't to talk you out of "climbing the ladder," but to help you enjoy and appreciate the journey more no matter what kind of path you take.

Living near your center also gives you a different perspective on your achievements. In my life I've been lucky enough to reach many of the goals I set for myself (although to be fair, there have also been a few that I've either missed out on or haven't gotten to yet).

The feeling of standing on stage and receiving a professional award, flying a helicopter with the doors off and the ground screaming below you at tree-top level, or diving a sunken wreck as a scuba instructor – as examples – can be exhilarating. Ultimately, though, what really made me happy about each of these pursuits was the journey it took to get there. The trip really *is* more important than the destination. The closer you get to your center, the more you become aware of that... and the more you enjoy your life as a consequence.

In order to find your center, you want to carry that feeling of sharing in a meaningful way with you on a regular basis. You want to feel as though the work you're doing and the time you're spending matter, which is virtually impossible when you are only focused on your own achievements, your own wealth, or your own status.

As humans, we are incredibly malleable. What we think or believe about ourselves from one day to the next isn't constant; it shifts with our moods, experience, and education. If you only trust and believe in yourself, then your sense of stability is always moving, too. That can lead to an uneasy feeling, and one that men and women who are too self-involved often try to dull with things like alcohol, drugs, and unhealthy relationships. Each of these, in turn, takes you farther from your center, and away from that feeling of happiness and excitement that every person craves.

On a more tangible level, having a larger perspective teaches us empathy and understanding, which can make us stronger, more effective people. If you never gain the ability to see the world from a point of view that isn't your own – and one that isn't colored by your own thoughts, feelings, and motivations – then you aren't just missing the bigger picture, you're also missing a big opportunity.

Faith Keeps You Grounded

Throughout history, faith has been a psychological and spiritual rock that humans have been able to use to guide themselves and each other through tough times. It all comes back to the fact that believing in something outside of your own life and your own abilities is naturally grounding. It stops you from losing your worldview when things start to seem topsy-turvy, as they often do.

Without faith in some sort of greater good or higher power, it's very easy to find yourself drifting off from one idea or inspiration to the next, because you don't have the kind of perspective that will keep you rooted. Conversely, when you *do* have a strong sense of faith, it's very difficult for anyone or anything to make you doubt your purpose.

To see how this works in the real world, I'll take you to another historical example. This time I want to focus on Corrie ten Boom, a Dutch woman whose family hid Jewish neighbors from the Nazis during World War II.

Her family's involvement in the Dutch underground began with the simple desire to help a neighbor find his way to safety. Soon, though, word spread of what they'd done and more people came looking for help. Despite the fact that they were strangers, it meant grave danger for them, and there was little chance they'd ever get anything in return, Corrie's family started forming elaborate schemes to hide, feed, and protect Jewish refugees under their roof.

Over the course of several years, they personally touched dozens and dozens of lives until eventually the home was raided and the entire family was sent to a concentration camp. There, Corrie's father died and she experienced firsthand the kinds of horrors and atrocities that might have made many question their actions and beliefs. However, even amid the death and pain around her, she remained steadfast that she had done the right thing until she was eventually released a short time later. Afterward, she continued her charitable work, working with foster children and mentally disabled individuals throughout her life.

Obviously, there are a lot of elements of charity, kindness, and perseverance in her story, but what really stands out to me is the level of faith that someone has to have in their convictions to put their life at risk to stay true to their values. That's the kind of thing that can *only* happen when you are living near your center and don't feel the need to question whether you're making the right decisions or not.

For another, less dramatic example, we can look to famous inventors like Thomas Edison or the Wright brothers. Even though they started with little more than dreams, they had the faith to keep trying new things. Although Edison could have ended up bankrupt, and the Wright brothers could have been killed if their invention wasn't what they thought it was, they persisted through hundreds upon hundreds of small failures until they finally reached a breakthrough. That's the power of determination, and an illustration of what you can accomplish when you have faith in a positive outcome on your side.

> **With faith, humans can cure diseases, find the strength to fight against tyranny, and walk on the moon… without it, the smallest setback will leave you filled with the kind of self-doubt that stops you from accomplishing anything at all.**

Faith Leads to Inner Peace

One thing you may have noticed in this discussion on faith is that, by giving you something to turn to outside of yourself, you can use faith to become grounded and find direction. That, in turn, gives you peace of mind that's impossible to achieve any other way.

A friend of mine flew planes in the Navy long ago, at a time when modern navigation tools like GPS fell firmly into the category of "science fiction." In fact, a lot of areas weren't even covered by radar at the time. In those days, it wasn't entirely unheard of for planes to get lost and disappear for a while, especially if there was bad weather that could prevent the crew from being able to pick up on things like visual cues and radio transmissions.

This retired pilot likes to tell about how, when flying back then, you could make a flight plan, and even adjust for things like wind, but you needed to have another point of reference to ever be sure exactly where you were at any given moment. It didn't matter if it was a radio navigation signal, an identifiable point on a map, or even a star constellation that you knew the direction of – you just had to have something that could help you figure out where you were above the earth's surface, and whether you had drifted far from your course.

In this life, faith is that reference point. Knowing that there's something else out there, even if it's just the shared human experience, is necessary to move forward with any confidence. When you know that you're supporting your bigger goals, and that your life is on target, you don't have to stare at the map endlessly. When you feel lost without any reference point, on the other hand, any direction seems as good as the others because you aren't sure where you're headed.

In that way, only faith can lead you to true peace of mind. Some might argue that you can actually find peace of mind without it, but that's a different sort of sensation altogether.

> **Real peace of mind comes from knowledge and insight. Not caring isn't the same thing. One comes from faith; the other arises from being numbed to the world or ignorant of what's going on around you.**

For a quick explanation of the difference, think of a person who has consumed mind-altering drugs and is "blissed out." They might seem to have peace of mind, in the sense that they aren't concerned about their life direction (or anything else), but what they have is a false sense of security that ultimately is going to lead to more anxiety later. When you have strong faith, you don't have to worry that your peace of mind is false, or that it's going to wear off later, because you feel firm in your hard-won convictions.

Finding Your Own Faith

If you already have a great deal of faith in your life, whether it's religious or not, then using that to keep yourself closer to center probably won't be a challenge. In fact, it might be something that has helped you remain calm and close to your purpose through difficult times in the past.

If that's the case, I would encourage you to think about your faith, how you could make it stronger, and how to make it a part of your core value system that you regularly feed and encourage. Over time, that will make your faith a source of mental and emotional strength when you need it.

However, if you would consider yourself to be the kind of person who doesn't have any faith or spirituality, then I hope you'll go through this section and see how a little change in perspective might help you find that centered feeling that we are all trying to reach.

To that end, the first step might be wondering if you don't already have more faith than you think. Most of us do. After all, spirituality isn't just a habit, but it's a characteristic of people throughout the ages that is common across all cultures. Historically, mankind has always found meaning in the world and our lives, even if it wasn't expressed in a religious way.

How else would you define the burials that the earliest humans gave each other? If those ancient wanderers had truly believed that there was nothing more to life than what could be seen, smelled, and tasted, they wouldn't have bothered interring one another into the ground. And later, kings and pharaohs wouldn't have built monuments if not for the abiding belief that it's important for humans to make their mark and establish a legacy.

In our own time, even though fewer people identify themselves as religious, only a very small minority would be so cynical as to claim they don't have faith in anything. Whether it's in the power of love, the strength of family, or even national pride, we all tend to gravitate toward those ideals and beliefs that we hold dear. In this way, faith and values are intertwined – not only do they move together in our minds and souls, but without them each of us would be nothing more than a blank slate.

Throughout my life, I have personally experienced the importance of faith. It has helped me to get through my darkest times, to be sure, but also to find more meaning and joy in life's triumphs.

When I was still a teenager, a very close friend of mine passed away in a swimming accident right before my eyes. Although this was long before I thought of the concepts in this book at any length, I remember how devastated I was, and the difference working together with a spiritual advisor made in my life at that point. I needed that faith to get through an incredibly difficult time and to be able to find the meaning and closure I needed to move forward.

Later in life, my faith helped me to form and appreciate personal relationships on a deeper level. It has impacted the way I think about my wife, my kids, and those closest to me. Having faith in something bigger made each of these bonds even more special.

Strengthening Your Beliefs

If you'll accept that almost everyone has *some* sort of faith, regardless of how strong or traditional that might be, then finding the spiritual component to your center becomes quite a bit easier. In the same way that you might use exercise to strengthen your physical stamina and endurance, for example, you can actually strengthen your faith and make it a source of peace and comfort through practice. All you really have to do is find where your faith lies, and then learn to trust in what you can sense but not see.

I hope that I have been able to persuade you to search for a bit of belief in *something* if you don't have it already. The world is a tough place, no matter how close to your center you are at any given moment. Faith is the anchor that keeps you from being blown away when the winds of change and chaos start to inevitably blow in your face.

CHAPTER FIVE

The Five Tenets of Center

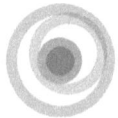

To this point, we've talked about what your center is, but we haven't explored in very much detail how to reach it. The secret is structuring your life in a way that is in alignment with five important tenets that keep you in equilibrium.

Before we get to the actual tenets themselves, I should take a moment to point out they aren't rules or commitments, just the cornerstones of a successful, fulfilling life. They are the qualities and characteristics that the most driven, inspired, and contented people have – the magic ingredients that allow people to display traits like kindness, humility, and perseverance, qualities of a centered life that we'll be looking at in a coming chapter.

Additionally, although you can consider them individually, it's important to remember that they work best in conjunction and coordination with one another. Having three without the other two, for example, will never leave you feeling fully satisfied. And, emphasizing a few over the others is always going to create problems in your life, as well (a point we will return to a little bit later).

If you wanted to illustrate these tenets a different way, there are a lot of unique analogies you can draw upon. You could compare them to major food groups, each of which is necessary to feel healthy and energized. Or, if you prefer, you could consider them like separate parts of a company, working together for manufacturing, sales, customer service, and so on, to create a healthy enterprise. You could even compare them to different players on a sports team, fulfilling different roles so that bigger objectives can be met.

You probably have the idea by now. And things will become even clearer as we move through each of the tenets, and how they work together.

Here are the five areas of your life that we'll be focusing on:
- Your Inner Circle
- Financial Harmony
- Values Alignment
- Spiritual Awareness
- Purpose and Direction

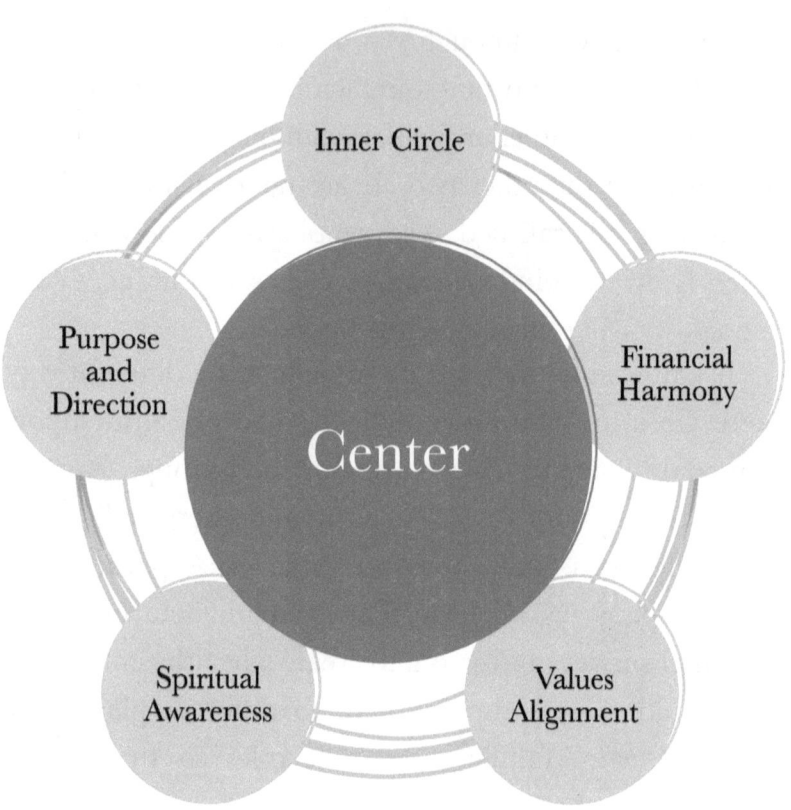

As you read through them, remember that these aren't just words on a page, but components of *your life* that greatly contribute to your sense of happiness and well-being. For that reason, I want to challenge you to identify your strengths and weaknesses and to look for the tenets that you are handling well and those that you could be paying more attention to.

Additionally, I encourage you to take a bit of time thinking of these both individually and as a whole. At first glance, you might think there are some cornerstones of a happy or successful life that are missing. As you move through each section, though, I think you'll find that the "missing" tenets are actually subsets of the five you'll see here, especially when it comes to personal values and priorities.

In other words, as in all things, keep an open mind. These tenets work because they draw on factors that are all part of the human condition. They don't just matter in my life or yours, but in everyone's.

Your Inner Circle

For a lot of people, an "inner circle" will essentially amount to family. This shouldn't be any surprise, as family tends to be a top priority for many, if not most, of the world's most successful people. In fact, you probably have many friends and contacts who would consider family to be the most important priority in their lives.

So, why not just say "family"? The difference between family and an inner circle represents a simple but crucial distinction – although having loved ones in your life, and making time for them, is incredibly important to your well-being, those loved ones don't have to technically be your family.

Some people form far closer bonds with their friends than they do their family members because they naturally feel more at ease with them. Others might not have any family at all, either because they've been lost or weren't there in the first place. And of course, there are some people who have lots of family, but don't find those relationships to be positive or supportive.

While the loss of family (or not feeling close to the family you have) can certainly create hardships, it doesn't have to keep you from your center. That's because the bonds we form with other people are what matter, not necessarily the blood ties or genetic material we have in common. In this sense, having a big family isn't necessarily better than knowing dozens of acquaintances at the office; you need people around you that you care about, and to have someone you know care about you.

Regardless of how you define your inner circle, or who is inside it, these relationships can be an enormous source of strength, support, and perspective. As I once heard it said, without significant others you can't know how significant you really are. Anyone who's ever been through an extremely difficult period in their lives knows how important it is to have someone who sympathizes, understands, and is pulling for you. Actually, anyone who's ever gone through a rough patch *without* that kind of support knows it even more.

To see evidence of how innate this yearning to find companionship with others really is, you only have to look at the psychological crisis we often find men and women going through in the Internet age. Even though the world is more "connected" than it's ever been in the past, there are a lot of people who feel terribly alone. They'll seek out friends, partners, and associates wherever they can find them. Some find a sense of community in Internet chat rooms; others spend long hours in bars or hang out with people they know are bad influences just to avoid being alone.

In extreme circumstances, young people may even join gangs just to feel like they're part of a bigger group, or at least that they belong. From the outside, these behaviors might seem strange and destructive, but to lonely people they make perfect sense. Whether it's having people around you to lift you up when you feel at your worst or just feeling energized by others you enjoy spending your time with, our social circles impact our entire lives. Without them, we often feel exhausted mentally, physically, and spiritually.

For that reason, part of this tenet is having an inner circle that you can count on, but another part is prioritizing. Most of us learn pretty early in our lives how easy it is to take our loved ones for granted. We generally don't appreciate our parents when we're young, ignore the fact that our siblings or best friends will likely move away at some point, and assume that our closest companions will always be near our side, when the truth is almost always the opposite.

Aside from making time for our loved ones simply because they matter to us, it's important for our well-being (and theirs) that we don't let them take a constant backseat to our careers, hobbies, and other competing priorities. If you ignore your inner circle, the people in it might eventually go away. When that happens, you'll almost undoubtedly wish that they hadn't. And you'll have missed out on one of the biggest ingredients to a happy, fulfilled life.

Looking back, I can still vividly remember the fear and uneasiness I felt when I was leaving for my first Army deployment. I had never been outside the country and was headed to Europe for two years. I would be away from my home, my family, and virtually everyone I knew for the first time in my life, and it was causing me an enormous amount of stress.

Just when it all seemed overwhelming, I had a moment to spend alone with my father at the airport. He sensed that my nerves were on edge and gave me a piece of advice that I've never forgotten: "You can't get finished until you get started."

Those simple words have helped guide me through my life and offer just a small example of the many ways my inner circle has given me the strength and comfort I needed to get past challenges and roadblocks.

You probably have similar memories, as well. Even though most of us tend to rely on our inner circle when times are tough, the reality is that they make every day easier to live in… and our lives more worth living.

When it comes to finding your center, closeness matters but exact relationships don't. You don't have to have a large family, or even a significant other – you just have to have others who are significant to you.

> **With those relationships, others in your life are constantly pulling you toward center; without them, the search for meaningful connections will always pull you away from your center.**

SEARCHING FOR CENTER

- *Which people are most important in your life?*

- *Can you think of three or four times in your life when your inner circle was especially supportive to you?*

- *Do you have people in your inner circle now who aren't as positive or supportive as they could be?*

Financial Harmony

Even though few topics are ever thought and written about as much as money, you might be surprised to find a reference to finances in a book about seeking your mental, emotional, and spiritual center. After all, isn't money supposed to not matter in the bigger scheme of things? Shouldn't spirituality come without a price tag?

Both of those sentiments are certainly accurate in a big-picture sense. When it comes to day-to-day living, though, we all know that money can be a huge priority, and even a distraction or preoccupation. It's true that your spirit has nothing to do with your finances, but it's *also* true that it's difficult to listen to your inner self when you're always thinking about money.

In the journey to find your center, financial harmony really amounts to a two-sided topic: On the one hand, it's much easier to think about yourself and your life clearly when you're able to meet your immediate needs. On the other hand, however, spending too much of your focus and attention on money can be damaging. Without it, you have persistent needs and concerns that aren't being taken care of, and with too much of it (or too much *emphasis* on it), you miss out on more important things.

To the first point, we'll return to basic psychology. If you're familiar with Maslow's hierarchy of needs, you've already seen his observation that you can't self-actualize (move close to your center) if you're constantly worried about where your next meal will come from. A complete lack of adequate financial resources will almost always leave you worried about things like food and shelter, which can be very counterproductive when you're trying to find your center of calm and peace.

What's interesting about this, though, is how relative it can all be. That's why I'm careful to use words like *adequate* and *almost*. My needs might not be the same as your needs, and the more focused you are on other parts of your life – and the less concerned you are with material things – the easier it might be for you to meet those day-to-day necessities.

To that point, a person with very little money can actually be in financial harmony, if only because they have learned to let go of their anxiety about material possessions. Consider Mother Teresa. Although she didn't accumulate any wealth, she was certainly in a position of financial harmony in her life because she wasn't ever preoccupied with earnings and investments.

While I'm certainly not advising you to give up everything you own, this leads us to the second element of financial harmony, which is being satisfied with what you have once it's enough to meet your needs. That doesn't mean you can't earn or accumulate more, of course, just that it shouldn't be your primary motivation past a certain point.

A wise man once told me that money comes in two amounts, "enough" and "not enough." Besides being witty, that statement hides an underlying but important truth.

> **Most of us learn at some point or another that earning more money seems like an easy way to permanently improve our lives, but that viewpoint rarely turns out to be valid.**

For one thing, the activities or life changes that would be required of us to actually earn that money might make the reality much different from the fantasy. And for another, the world is full of people who are incredibly rich and just as incredibly unhappy. Having more doesn't always mean living better, and in fact sometimes means enjoying everything a little bit less.

Besides, if you leave your primary focus on money, you don't have room for the other important things in your life. There isn't much point to earning more money if you aren't enjoying it, and staring too hard at a set of numbers and letting them define you can actually pull you away from your center pretty quickly.

SEARCHING FOR CENTER

- *How much money would be enough for you to feel satisfied?*

- *What would it take for you to enjoy more financial harmony?*

- *How could you use some of your financial resources to bring more happiness to your life and the lives of others?*

VALUES ALIGNMENT

In a coming chapter, I am going to ask you to think carefully about your own values, since those values make up parts of your personality that have to be expressed if you're going to live at or near your center. In some cases, your values may coincide closely with the tenets we are describing here, or with the idea of faith and spirituality that are so important to this concept.

What makes your values different, though, is that they are uniquely your own. While a lot of people *tend* to have similar values and beliefs, a lot of them come down to your own needs and preferences. That's why I will encourage you to look into accepted assessment tools, and to do some brainstorming, in order to come up with your own.

For example, one of my values is adventure. When I don't pay attention to this element in my life, I start to get a bit irritable and feel "off." Adventure might not be important to you at all, but I'm willing to bet that something else that isn't on my list of values matters a great deal to your happiness.

Regardless of what your specific values are, or what parts of your life you value the most, you need to live in a way that's in alignment with them if you're going to find your center. Otherwise, you'll have the sense that something is missing, and that you're fighting against your own inner priorities.

Often, this is what people mean when they complain about "selling out," even though the decisions that they are making might have nothing to do with money – the real problem is that they don't feel like they are living or working in a way that lines up with their personal values, and it's painful on a mental and spiritual level. It's like sand in an engine, causing friction with every action or movement. Working against your values harms your creativity, saps your energy, and leaves you with the nagging feeling that you're dragging yourself in the wrong direction.

A similar problem can occur when you have different values that are in conflict with one another. For example, it could be that one of your values is sharing, while another is reaching positions of power. Or, it could be that a value for adventure goes against a value of caring for our families. How much personal risk is *too much* risk when it's also the future of our loved ones that's on the line?

As you might've guessed, the answer is once again going to be extremely personal. Someone who is the CEO of a large company might have a different value for personal power than I do, just as an Olympic downhill skier is going to think about personal risk in a way you or I don't. The only answer is to study ourselves, think on the issue consciously and unconsciously, and then start to make priorities. Sometimes our values aren't going to be perfectly aligned. That's all right because life is messy and all of our wishes and dreams don't fit into neat little boxes that can be stacked on top of one another. But, by paying close attention to these issues and deciding what really matters most, we can find answers that work for us.

I also want to point out that many of our values aren't conscious desires or things that we would express out loud. Something like the need for power and authority, the fear of loss, etc., could be an especially powerful unconscious motivator for you. Most of us have one or more aspects of our personality that are like that, sitting beneath the surface. That doesn't mean that we are somehow evil or duplicitous, just that we need to be aware of our own inner traits, even if they aren't obvious on a conscious level.

> **It should be obvious that living in alignment with our values is critical to finding center, if only because we see so many people who aren't doing either.**

When you aren't paying attention to your inner beliefs and priorities, that's going to create a lot of problems for you eventually. It's much better to know what they are and build a life that incorporates all of them.

SEARCHING FOR CENTER

- *Which parts of your life are most in or out of alignment with your values?*

- *Do you have any personal values that are in conflict with one another?*

- *Are there any major changes you need to make to live in a way that's consistent with your personal values?*

SPIRITUAL AWARENESS

As with your personal values, spirituality is something that we've spent a substantial bit of time on in this book, both because it's so important to finding your center and because it's something that isn't usually understood or discussed often enough out in the open.

Assuming that you have followed along so far and are willing to admit that each of us has a spiritual side, you probably recognize that your spirituality can provide a sense of rootedness and perspective that is impossible to fake or duplicate. Conversely, if you aren't aware of your spirituality, then you're likely to question your own beliefs and direction constantly because you don't have any faith in them.

This is true even for people who think they aren't spiritual. All of us are continually being acted on by forces and dimensions that we aren't consciously aware of. In this case I'm not talking about hidden planes of awareness or a secret spirit world; instead, I'm referring to simple forces like time and gravity.

As you read this on a page or screen, time is continually flowing on and on at a continual rate. And, gravity is holding you into your chair, even if you aren't paying attention to it. In fact, the same would be true even if you had never heard of concepts like gravity or time. You would be aware of their effects, even if you couldn't explain them. I could make the same argument for things like light, heat, or microbial bacteria. Doubting their existence and effects won't stop you from being pushed or pulled in a number of different directions.

Imagine for a second that you were a very small ant, sitting on a long sheet of paper. At that moment, you might perceive a world that is essentially two-dimensional, stretching out almost infinitely in every direction. Now, imagine that some sort of weight or pressure is applied to the center of the paper, ever so slightly. Even though your world still seems two-dimensional, you are very likely to find that any forward movement you make brings you toward that pressure in the middle.

That explanation is one professors use to demonstrate how gravity works in a non-mathematical sense. But it applies to the topic at hand, as well. In the same way that gravity draws physical matter in, your spiritual side exerts a force over your life, too, regardless of whether or not you're aware of that extra dimension. Just like time and gravity are moving you in one direction, your spirituality is either pulling you toward your center or away from it. The difference is largely how aware you are of your spirit, and whether you have faith in something that can guide you in the right direction.

On a more tangible level, a lack of spirituality and faith removes that reference point that I discussed in an earlier chapter. Once that's gone, it's easy to find yourself looking for the wrong purpose in your life (something we will look at in a moment), ignoring your inner circle, or losing your sense of financial harmony because you're too focused on the material world.

> **Without accepting some form of faith in a higher power, religious or not, you don't have an anchor to hold you near your center, especially when things get tough.**

SEARCHING FOR CENTER

- *Is your spiritual belief system giving you strength and perspective when you need it most?*

- *How much attention do you pay to the spiritual side of your life?*

- *Are you letting the term "religion" distract you from a connection to your sense of spirituality? If so, what can you do to change it?*

Your Purpose and Direction

What is your true purpose? What is it that you're really built to do?

More often than not, the answer to these types of questions comes down to the intersection between joy and talent. That is, most of us perform at our very best when we are in a position to do something we love and also happen to be very good at. For some, like athletes and artists, recognizing one's purpose can be easy and obvious; for others, it takes a bit of work.

Part of the confusion comes from the fact that your purpose isn't necessarily a job title or career path. Some people naturally gravitate toward teaching and coaching, for example, but that can encompass a very wide range of paths. Conversely, we all know natural leaders and entertainers, but those are skills that are valuable to several different professions and hobbies, as well.

Attaching importance to your purpose is easy. When you know where your greatest strengths and most important life goals lie, you can find work and activities that are fulfilling and rewarding. You feel like you're contributing something meaningful, and you are enjoying yourself at the same time.

With that realization, what matters most isn't that you decide how you should be earning your income (although finding your true purpose will often lead you toward a fulfilling career), but that you identify your inherent talents and make the most of them. In other words, you allow your best self to come forward.

> **Finding your purpose is about self-discovery, not self-invention. In other words, you figure out where your talents and aspirations already lie, not try to create them on your own. You don't try to be something you're not, no matter how green the grass seems on some other side (or in some other personality or career path).**

That might seem a little bit limiting, but in truth it's incredibly liberating. Far, far too many of us are living lives that we don't really enjoy simply because we want to be a different way than we actually are, or think that we would find more acceptance if we developed different dreams or talents. The reality, though, is that the farther we turn from our own nature, the more frustrated we become.

And so, if you want to reach your center, you need to find your purpose or direction. Doing so will probably help you in more ways than you could possibly imagine. That's because you'll feel less stress about the things you do, will achieve more, and will be more respected by those you work with.

Like most of the core topics in this book, finding your focus is largely about paying attention to your own self. Some of the insight can be gained from aptitude tests, but you can often find what you need to know by looking into your past and seeing where you truly excelled. Experimenting with a trial-and-error approach can also be helpful – if you follow a hunch, it might lead you to talents you didn't know were there.

No one feels good doing a job that they are ill suited for, or performing a role that goes against their nature. Whether you're a leader or a follower, an introvert or an extrovert, a creative thinker or an analytic, there is a place for you in this world. You were designed for some essential purpose. That shouldn't be your whole identity, of course, but you shouldn't try to ignore it or contradict it, either.

Note that your true purpose can actually be independent of your career path altogether. For an obvious example of why this can be, consider the case of someone who retires but still has a lot of energy left to pursue different causes or interests. Even though that person's *purpose* might not have changed, the specific *role* they fill, or outlet they use to fulfill it, could be completely different than it once was. Leaders who were executives become mentors; organizers who earned salaries as accountants can become nonprofit board members. Business owners can turn into youth league coaches.

The same kind of process can happen as we evolve from one point or position to another. Your purpose (or multiple purposes) will likely remain constant, but in our changing world, most of us have short-term titles and aspirations that are often in flux.

Recently, I had the privilege to sit next to a gentleman on a long flight who was just approaching his 90th birthday. Our conversation began casually, but he went on to tell me about his life in England as a college student during World War II. He had served in the so-called "bucket brigade," putting out fires throughout the blitz and helping to save countless others in the process.

Not only did he survive, but went on to thrive and achieve enormous levels of success throughout his adult life, and in fact well into what many would have considered to be his "retirement years."

At 89 years old, he continues to consult with a great deal of energy and passion. So, rather than spending his days playing cards or sitting in front of a television, he travels over 100,000 airline miles per year.

Obviously, this isn't the kind of path for every person to take. But, what will always be memorable to me is the way this man knew his purpose and redefined his role again and again. He recognized that change didn't have to mean giving up who he was or what he loved, and made the most of his talents in a number of interesting ways.

SEARCHING FOR CENTER

- *Do you feel like the life you live is a good match for your skills, talents, and desires?*

- *Does success in your chosen field (or your most prominent personal activities) make you feel proud and fulfilled?*

- *If you are at or nearing retirement, how can you repurpose your life for the next phase of your life?*

Finding Balance Among the Five Tenets

Earlier in this chapter, I asked you to think about the five tenets of center as being three-dimensional. Now, I want to go a bit further and ask you to think of each one as a leg on a five-sided table or stool. The minute you shorten any one of them, or eliminate one altogether, your situation becomes a lot less stable than it was before. You certainly can't sit comfortably without all the legs of the stool in place, and it's going to be very easy for you to topple over if they aren't holding you up.

That's kind of a simplistic way of looking at things, but it nicely illustrates the need for balance among the tenets of center. If you don't have financial harmony in your life, you're always looking for more money, regardless of the personal and professional costs. If you lack spiritual awareness, you can't develop the kind of faith that will bring you peace and perspective. Life feels empty without your inner circle, going against your values causes internal friction, and a lack of purpose will leave you drifting and unfulfilled.

It's just as important to realize that you can't *over*-emphasize any one of the tenets, either. Too much of anything isn't good for you. This is actually even more insidious because putting all of your attention on one tenet can lead you to think you're doing "good" things, or the "right" things, even though you're really pulling yourself away from your center.

Balance is critical because life changes. Some changes can be foreseen and others can't, but they all occur every day. Presidents become ex-presidents; executives become consultants or job seekers; CEOs turn into amateur golf experts. In each case, a role or position that could be self-defining – even if it's a good one – can lead to problems if balance isn't a priority. Without any other identity, or the other tenets to fall back on, one single event could throw an unbalanced person wildly out of center.

Note that I haven't always gotten this right in my own life. Like the cliché stressed-out ER doctor who used to smoke, or the dentist with an insatiable sweet tooth, I have had to learn to practice what I preach more than once. That's because, like a lot of us, I have occasionally found myself devoting too much time and energy into one area of my life – at the expense of others that are just as important.

For relatively short periods of time I've gotten so wrapped up in my career, for example, that I've failed to give my inner circle and spiritual focus the attention they needed. Thankfully, using the same concepts I outlined in this book, I've been able to "recalibrate" my thinking and get back to what really matters. And in the process, I've moved myself back toward center. By emphasizing balance in your life, you can do the same.

Later, we are going to look at how life circumstances can change your center, and alter the priorities or definitions you put on your individual tenets.

> **But, regardless of where you are in your life at the moment, you should remain conscious of these five cornerstones of a happy, fulfilled life. All of them matter, and balance is the key.**

It's only when all five are in place that you can sit comfortably at or very near to your center.

SEARCHING FOR CENTER

- *Can you identify any particular tenets of center that stand out the most in your mind for being fulfilled or unfulfilled?*

- *Do you have something that's going very well in your life or something that you feel is missing from your life?*

- *Which tenets of center are you spending most of your time and energy on?*

CHAPTER SIX

Qualities of People Who Are Near Center

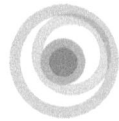

*E*ven if you don't feel like you're living near your center at the moment, you probably know someone who is. In fact, even if you've never thought about it in those terms, there are probably people you admire in your life simply because they seem focused, composed, and content.

We *all* tend to know people like this. That's partly because they tend to gravitate toward leadership positions, or become authorities in their chosen fields even if they aren't very outgoing by nature. Another reason, however, is that people who are centered tend to have an attractive quality about them. I don't necessarily mean that they are attractive in the romantic sense, but that they draw others to them because they are driven, confident, and easy to be around. You can sense a completeness in the way they live.

> **You'll notice there can sometimes be an enormous difference between those who are *centered* and those who are *professionally successful*.**

Although the two often go hand-in-hand, you can make lots of money, find a position of power, and even be admired within your field without being near your center. That's not an enjoyable way to live, of course, but there are millions of people who are succeeding in their careers while failing in virtually every other part of their lives. We might respect them, but we certainly don't want to emulate them.

When we meet people who are living at their center, on the other hand, we are inspired by their seemingly complete success. We want to learn their secret and make it our own. That can be important because it drives us to seek center in our own lives. It makes us want the peace, confidence, and creativity we see in others. Also, when we see others at or near their center, we identify those who can serve as mentors to us in our own journey, which is something we will explore later in the book.

For now, though, we'll take a closer look at each of the traits that are common to people who are living very near their center:

Self-Discipline	Integrity	Perseverance
Charity	Humility	Kindness

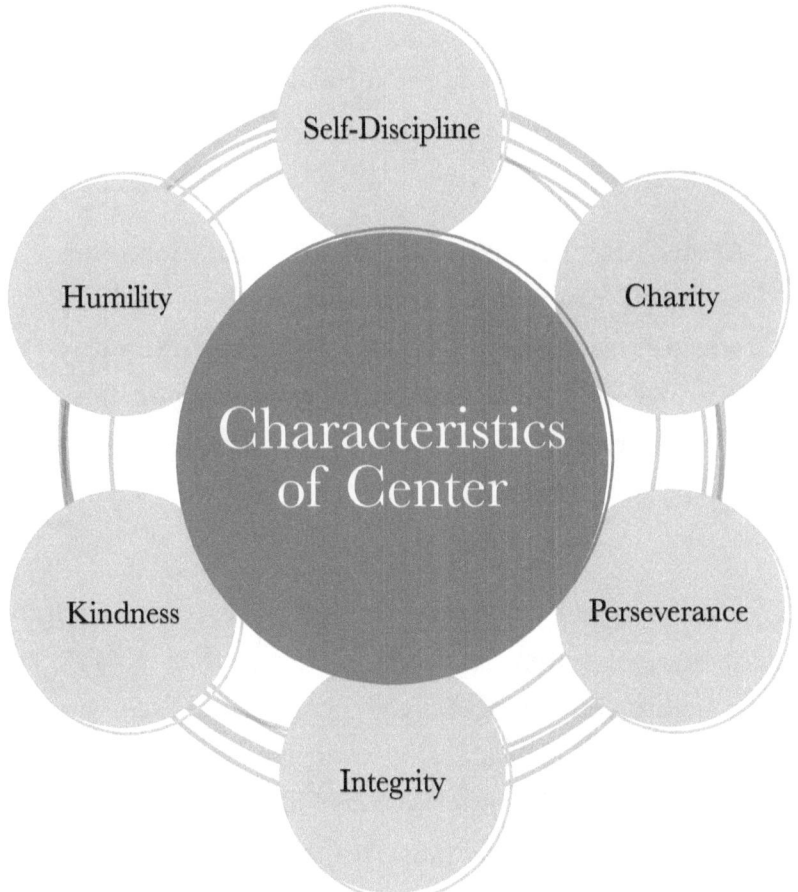

Each of these qualities is important to being effective and to staying near your center. Of course, the distinctions between them are a little bit arbitrary – you'll probably realize right away that most of them go together in some way or another, and that people who have one quality usually have most of the others, as well.

Let's look at each of these qualities in a little more depth.

Self-Discipline

It probably won't come as any surprise that self-discipline is a common trait among people who are at their center.

> **After all, having the ability to motivate yourself toward a particular goal, especially when it isn't easy, is required for virtually any kind of success... and men and women who live near their center are by definition almost always successful.**

On a deeper level, discipline is even more important to the process of self-evaluation and change that has to take place before you can actually feel centered. Learning who you are, and what you really want, can be frustrating to many, and especially those who feel like they have taken a few "wrong turns" in the past. At the same time, old habits and ideas are easy to fall back into, which means changing thoughts and behaviors has to involve discipline.

There aren't going to be many external forces in your life that are going to move you toward your center – but there will probably be dozens that can pull you away. Self-discipline, the strength that comes with being driven from inside, is what's going to make all the difference.

Unfortunately, self-discipline is becoming a rare commodity in our world. Many of us simply feel as if we don't have the strength to do the things we need to do, or to see through the small and large changes we wish to effect in our lives.

For an easy illustration of this phenomenon, consider the New Year's resolutions that millions upon millions of us make each and every January. Surveys show the vast majority of people – more than 95% – won't ever reach their resolutions. They have a yearning for a different life, or at least a new set of habits, but just can't seem to reach what they desire. This tendency doesn't just affect their ability to start and finish important projects, but can also potentially color their own esteem and self-respect. It's hard to reach your center, or even feel good about your life, if you feel like you don't have the strength to make changes when they are needed.

What they need to know, and what might help you to boost your own self-discipline as you seek center, is that there are two easy ways to gain more drive and achieve more of what you want to. The first is by simply starting small. Just get into the habit of setting simple targets for yourself (like reading an inspirational book for 10 minutes, or walking half a mile after work each day) and then following through. Although these little bits of progress might seem meaningless at first, they'll lead to a bigger sense of confidence and achievement that will make you more disciplined over time.

Another way to build up your self-discipline is to begin with an *external* motivation first. This is something we see frequently in men and women who've been in the military. Although their discipline was originally imposed by someone else (like a drill sergeant or commanding officer) for a long time, most of them *stay* motivated and disciplined after they leave the service. What was an obligation becomes a habit.

You can do the same without going to basic training; all you need is another person to help out. For example, if you have an important project due soon, find a colleague you can meet with on a regular basis to discuss it. You won't want to show up at these meetings having done nothing, so you're likely to change your habits and start making progress right away. Or, you could spend money to hire a personal trainer at the gym or a professional coach who will work with you after hours at the office. They'll hold you accountable for your habits in a similar way. You could even do the same thing with friends, colleagues, or family members who know what you're trying to achieve and can check up on you.

Over time, these external motivators will help change your habits, which in turn will lead to more self-discipline. You'll develop habits that you'll want to stick to, which will make you stronger and more driven to achieve your goals. Self-discipline isn't instilled overnight, but if you're willing to put in a little bit of time and effort, you can become one of the 5% who actually achieves their New Year's resolutions and other goals each year – and you'll be one step closer to reaching your center.

Perseverance

Perseverance and self-discipline go together closely, if only because you'll never have one without the other. And yet, they are actually distinct qualities. Both are important if you're ever going to become a high achiever at any level, or to reach your mental and spiritual center.

In this context, perseverance really just refers to *having the strength to keep going*. There isn't really anything complicated about perseverance, but that doesn't mean it's a quality that everyone possesses. In fact, it's remarkable to see how many people will give up on important goals and dreams simply because they find achieving them to be too much of an effort, or because they encounter some sort of obstacle they didn't expect or envision when they started out.

It's hard to ever find your center without perseverance, because mental and spiritual obstacles are almost bound to show up on a daily basis. And, it's probably impossible to live at or near your center without perseverance because life is always trying to throw problems and distractions at you when you need them least. No matter how strong your convictions are in the moment, your strength and faith are going to be tested time and time again. If you can persevere, these obstacles can be overcome; if you can't, it won't take much for you to lose your direction.

Strangely enough, the best way to turn yourself into the kind of person who can persevere is often to look for faith and purpose in your life – in other words, to move toward your center in other ways. That's because perseverance is really just a form of courage. It's the courage to believe things are going to be all right and that you're working toward the best possible outcome, even when the future seems in doubt. That's not an easy stance to take on, but when you have very strong values and convictions, and feel that you are well on the way to achieving your personal, professional, and spiritual goals, it becomes possible to minimize and move around setbacks and fears that start to come along.

Another key piece of advice when it comes to developing perseverance is to just crawl before you can walk. If you run into troubles that seem so overwhelming that you just don't know how to get past them, don't look for a big answer. Instead, identify the one small action you can take to get closer to your goal and do that. Once it has been completed, regardless of what happened as a result, use the same process again. Over time, you'll find that all of these small actions keep you reaching forward, even if it feels like you're crawling through thick mud. Sooner or later, progress will start to show itself, and that recognition will lead you to persevere even more.

Our world is filled with stories of people who persevered and overcame very long odds to do something that was important to them. We read all the time about athletes who have battled through injury, business leaders who went bankrupt and then built an empire all over again, and leaders who overcame huge losses in their personal lives only to come back stronger. You have the same strength inside of you, but not everyone knows where to find it.

> **If you make perseverance a priority, and exercise your faith in yourself and your values often enough, you'll discover that there really isn't anything that can hold you back.**

Once you gain that unstoppable feeling, you'll see why it's a big step toward finding your center.

INTEGRITY

In our world, integrity is a bit like a million dollars in cash. We all know that it's valuable, and we have a good idea of what it would look like, but don't see it nearly as often as we would like in our everyday lives.

For that reason alone, people who have a high degree of personal and professional integrity are admired and trusted by others. They just stand out because you know you can count on them to keep their word. And although most of us probably wouldn't ever take the time to think about it, a person with a high level of loyalty and integrity is also demonstrating that they have a strong sense of their internal values, along with the strength to stay true to them.

Conversely, people without a high degree of integrity are never fully trusted, regardless of the formal position or professional success they might achieve. Others sense a falseness about them and never truly commit to their ideas and visions. Even worse yet, these individuals know that they aren't trusted – and even that they can't trust themselves.

In the movies, integrity is shown (or alternatively, *not* shown) in big, dramatic moments as characters stand up for one another or show their true colors at the worst possible moment. In real life, though, things are rarely so cut and dried. Instead, we show our loyalty and integrity to others one small action and reaction at a time. We hold true to our personal principles even when it would be easier not to do so. We share credit with coworkers and colleagues when building ourselves up would be more advantageous. We refrain from saying the wrong things behind someone else's back, even if we can be reasonably sure they would never find out.

These are habits that don't just help you build strong character and become the kind of leader that others can respect – they also move you toward your center for the simple reason that they help you improve your self-image and become the kind of person you're meant to be. Or, to think about it another way, the habits help you support your underlying principles.

An easy way to understand this is by thinking about the vows you take when you get married. Regardless of whether you have a spouse or not, you're undoubtedly familiar with the expectation that, once you marry someone, you're going to cease having romantic relationships with other people.

If someone asks you to break that promise, you should of course make the right decision. But the *how* and *why* of that decision matter as much as the outcome does. If you don't do it because you're afraid of getting caught and losing half of your possessions, that's just a risk analysis. If you refrain because you believe it's the right thing to do, and because you love and respect your partner, then it becomes a matter of loyalty and integrity.

As you can imagine, the more you practice high standards of loyalty and integrity, the better you get at it and the better you feel about yourself. The principle applies in both directions; the more you practice *low* integrity, the worse you feel about yourself and the easier it is to repeat the mistake again and again in the future (and the farther you move from your center).

That means strengthening your integrity might require breaking a cycle if you aren't already in the habit of being loyal to others or to your own values. Luckily, this is usually pretty easy. First, you identify any areas in your life where you might feel like your integrity isn't being upheld. Those become conscious zones you can focus your attention on right away. Then, you make a point of reminding yourself about your values, integrity, and loyalty on a regular basis (through Post-it notes you've made to yourself, perhaps, or visual reminders around your home and office). Often, simply being more aware of your commitments, whether they were made to yourself or someone else, is enough to lead you to change your behavior.

> **We admire people who have loyalty and integrity because they represent something we should all aspire to in terms of personal strength. And, consciously or not, they show us how to use our actions and principles to move closer to center every day.**

CHARITY

People who are living near their center are always looking for ways to "give back," both in their communities and to others who are close to them. You can usually find them donating their time and attention to charitable causes, serving as mentors and team leaders at work, and offering what they can to others who need advice.

All of this is part of a charitable outlook on life, one that encompasses more than just their so-called "charity" time and donations. It isn't a coincidence that men and women near their center make the time and mental effort for these activities.

What they know, consciously or unconsciously through experience, is that you can't truly "give back" to anything or anyone, because you ultimately end up getting a lot more in return. Beyond the feeling you get when you're able to help someone else or contribute to an important cause, the act of practicing charity, or acting in a charitable way, is incredibly centering.

If you've ever spent an afternoon volunteering, or given money to a nonprofit you support, you probably already know why. The more you turn your attention toward doing the right things and on helping others to overcome their problems, the less mental space you have to worry about your own troubles. Additionally, acting in a charitable way often makes you appreciate what you have in your own life, which in turn reduces the materialistic wants and desires that can preoccupy us and pull us farther and farther from our center. And it gets you thinking about things that are more important than the day-to-day issues we all deal with, which is a positive thing for our perspective.

> **Acting charitably gives us more gratitude and increases our self-esteem. Both of these are great qualities for any person to have, and obviously allow us to feel more centered.**

And finally, when you behave charitably you put yourself in a position to be near others who are also living close to their center. The more of these men and women you have in your life, the stronger your support system will be, and the less chance there is that you'll start to experience self-doubts or be weighed down by negative thoughts, because you'll have the right examples all around you.

Charitable thinking and behavior is a habit, and one that any person can acquire regardless of their financial situation or scheduling demands. None of us is so busy that we don't have enough time to lend a hand when it's needed most or contribute to an important effort. Behaving in a charitable way doesn't have to be your whole life, and it doesn't necessarily need to involve working at a nonprofit, giving up the other things you love, or even serving on the boards of several different organizations – it's about a willingness to serve a cause that's bigger than your own life.

Developing a sense of charity is about more than just being nice, but the benefits are a lot bigger than the simple endorphin rush you get from donating a bit of money or spending a few hours at your local soup kitchen. When you truly make charity a part of your personality, and not just a series of activities you engage in from time to time, you make it much easier to experience a sense of warmth and fulfillment that pulls you closer to your spiritual center every day.

Humility

If you read the name of this trait and wondered to yourself whether humility had disappeared from the world, you probably aren't alone. Our society encourages self-promotion and attention-seeking behavior to the point of obnoxiousness; instead of being proud of our accomplishments, many of us are practically begging others to notice our achievements, even if they aren't that impressive or even entirely true.

And yet, the best way to stand apart in today's world is often by displaying just the smallest bit of humility about your work or attributes and letting your reputation speak for you. After all, when a person is truly confident, they don't need other people to recognize what they're doing or validate it. This is even more true for those who have discovered their real purpose. They aren't bothered about the opinions of other people who don't understand the path they're on because those opinions don't really matter.

> **Humility is much more than acting in a humble way, though, or letting your confidence come through. It's actually about recognizing that we are all in this together and that the human condition is universal.**

What you probably learned in kindergarten is still true today: Each person you meet is different, and we all have our own skills, talent, and knowledge. Regardless of what kind of education you have, every individual you'll ever come across knows many things that you don't. No matter how exceptional someone is in a particular field, or however much money they may have earned, there are things that you can do better than they can.

Coming to that knowledge, and treating all of the people as equals, is the essence of humility. It doesn't necessarily mean that you *like* everyone, but that you are able to treat them respectfully and look for those similarities.

Because humility is found in the absence of boasting and arrogance, it can be difficult to sense at first glance. A lack of humility, however, is often one of the first things you'll notice about someone who is off-center. Because of their lack of confidence, or lack of self-worth, they'll look for virtually *any* opportunity to put someone else down or to emphasize their dominance over another person. People with a high degree of humility look for intelligence and creativity anywhere they can find it; people without any humility refuse to recognize the merits of any thought or inspiration they didn't generate on their own.

Humility is necessary to reaching your center because you can't feel connected to others, or the world around you, if you're constantly putting yourself above other people. And, paradoxically enough, the more time you spend disrespecting others, the worse you tend to feel about yourself and your own life.

Even though developing humility might seem like a simple change in attitude, that's what can make it so difficult. After all, we all have egos, and those egos don't like any kind of negative feedback... even if it happens to be the truth. So give yourself a reality check once in a while and remember that, regardless of what success you may have had in the past, you aren't the ultimate authority on every topic, and your opinions aren't always right – just as they aren't worth less than the views of others who might be even more fortunate than you are.

The other great way to develop a humble personality is by surrounding yourself with others who have that quality. Often, the perspective you'll gain will be enough to show you how we are all connected. Once you realize that every human on the planet is in this together, you may find you have more humility than you thought.

Kindness

In many ways, practicing kindness is both easy and difficult. On the one hand, once you're actually near your center, being kind to others is often the easiest thing in the world because you already feel uplifted yourself. On the other hand, the farther you get from your center, the harder it is to behave in a kind way because you might feel jealous or resentful of other people.

But although kindness is easiest to display when you're already at or near your center, you can start practicing it regularly regardless of how you feel and add some joy to your life.

> **That's because the true basis of kindness shouldn't be that you want or expect someone to be kind to you in return. Instead, it's the recognition that, no matter what mood you're in or what you have going on in your life, others have the same issues and challenges to deal with, as well.**

In other words, it's not always about you, and the kindness you display to someone that you don't know, or who frankly might not even deserve it, can be the best thing for both of you. It makes you feel happier and centered to be kind to others, and the goodwill you spread can actually become infectious and contagious. Kindness has a way of spreading and growing once it has been released, especially when the kindnesses we give are unexpected.

Besides, kindness naturally springs from all of the other traits and practices we've already mentioned. The more you make an effort to be humble, for example, or become disciplined in your life, the more satisfied and content you feel... and the kinder and happier you feel as a result. It goes without saying that charity is its own form of kindness, and that those with a high degree of integrity find it easier to be nice to other people for the simple fact that they like themselves more.

This is all a way of saying that kindness is often a byproduct of happiness, which is in turn the natural result of being centered as a person. So, make a point to offer unexpected kindnesses to all the others you meet in your life, without any expectation that you're going to get something from them in return. You'll learn that kindness is its own reward, and that it's much easier to give as you get closer to your center.

Getting a Glimpse of Your Center

Hopefully, this chapter has helped to give names to some of the qualities you've already noticed in the most fulfilled people you know in your life, and given you some helpful ways that you might start to cultivate them on your own. Remember that the process of becoming centered is long and ongoing, so you shouldn't worry if you feel like you don't have these traits already. Most of us aren't nearly as disciplined, humble, or kind as we would like to be (or think we should be).

But, by knowing how a centered person looks and acts, we give ourselves something to strive for and start forming a picture in our minds of what a centered life might look like. And, we gain a way of thinking about the people we know that could lead us to find new mentors, friends, and advisors who can become very important to us later on.

These traits show us what being centered looks like from the outside. Finding your own center isn't just about changing a few attitudes or outward behaviors, though — it takes a journey inside your own mind and spirit that ultimately makes all of these other changes possible. In the next chapter, we'll see exactly how that works and what you can do to *really* make a difference in the way you feel about your life.

SEARCHING FOR CENTER

- *Who in your life is living at or near their center?*

- *What qualities do they have that you would like to make your own?*

- *What is it about their life that makes it most obvious that they're at their center?*

CHAPTER SEVEN

Values, Priorities, and Internal Clarity

*I*f finding your center is all about being engaged and fulfilled, then it only makes sense that the first step in our journey should be to figure out what really engages and fulfills you.

Strange as it might sound, these are issues a lot of men and women never really spend enough time thinking about. In fact, I sometimes get the distinct impression that dwelling on your own fulfillment is something that's almost looked down upon in some circles. If you spend too much time considering where your life is going, the thinking goes, you aren't devoting enough of your time and mental energy to actually accomplishing more and getting ahead.

Our "do it" society doesn't really inspire people to ask whether they're doing the right things to make themselves happy. Instead, financial and career "success" is supposed to cure all of what could possibly ail you.

That kind of circular logic doesn't work, of course, and we're going to tackle that in this chapter. It's time to find out what *really* drives you, since you'll never reach your center if you aren't sure what actually motivates you or makes you happy.

WHAT YOU WANT TO *DO* VERSUS WHO YOU WANT TO *BE*

Traditional goal-setting, career-planning, and lifestyle decision-making processes tend to focus on what we'd like to do or have at a given point in time. These kinds of targets can be helpful because they are tangible and easy to understand; either you've bought the new car or you haven't. The problem, however, lies in the fact that most of these cut-and-dried goals aren't indicative of the things that truly bring us joy.

This is a point so obvious it's almost cliché, but having a bigger salary, a better title on your business card, or an extra summer home won't ever lead to a permanent sense of contentment. That doesn't mean you shouldn't enjoy these things or that they aren't worthwhile, but rather that they represent symbols and symptoms of other things, like a sense of being financially comfortable, knowing that you are at the top of your profession, or having the freedom and flexibility to spend a lot of time with your loved ones.

It's important not to confuse the things with the attributes.

What we are talking about, of course, is confusing the forest for the trees in a very big way, and it's something that many of us have been guilty of at one time or another. But, if you really want to find your center, it's important to realize that you need to have a good sense of who you want to *be*, instead of focusing only on the things you want to *do* or *possess*.

To get to the heart of that, we need to move past that traditional, top-level layer of thinking and get to the values that are important to you.

The Value in Values

In the same way that spirituality often gets confused with religions and rituals, values tend to be seen as goals and notions that are necessarily lofty and obscure. While some of our values certainly can be expressed in those ways, the reality is that we aren't just talking about things that are important to you, or that you stand for. We're looking for what you're all about.

It goes without saying that values and priorities are going to differ from one individual to the next, but you should also know they can change, grow, or evolve from one time period to the next, as well. Very few of us have the same values at fifty that we had at fifteen; and for most of us, things can shift dramatically half a dozen times within that span.

Making things even more muddy is the fact that most of us never really take the time to actually define our values. We aren't used to expressing them, either to ourselves or others, so it's hard to actually put them into words when we try. To understand our own happiness, though, we have to understand ourselves first. Finding a set of values that moves us is important to doing that. Remember when I told you that finding your center wouldn't necessarily be easy? Most people, when they really take the time to think about it, find that their values aren't exactly what or where they thought they were.

Fortunately, there are several different steps you can take to discover yours, and none of them has to involve things like fasting or spending time alone in the wilderness. Instead, we're just going to get you to review your most important notions and beliefs one step at a time, beginning with the right questions...

It's Time to Put Yourself on the Spot

Suppose someone approached you at a dinner party and started asking you questions about your work or family. You wouldn't have any trouble finding answers, right? Now, imagine that they begin asking you about your deepest hopes and dreams. Beyond the awkwardness of sharing these insights with a stranger, you might find it difficult to even express what you're really feeling.

For that reason, a good first step is to ask yourself those same kinds of questions. Here are a few you can use to get the process started:

What kind of person do you really want to be?

As you look for the answer to this question, try not to focus on things like career goals or possessions. Instead, think of adjectives like strong, committed, generous, or focused. We're trying to get at the personality traits that are most important to you, whether you already have them or not.

What qualities do you admire in others?

Often, this is another way of discovering the answer to the first question. While you might not be able to express who you want to be, exactly, chances are you can spot it in others. For instance, if you love people who are brave and take risks, but have always considered yourself to be meek, that's an important insight.

How did (or do) your heroes act and behave?

Taking things a step further, consider what you love about your heroes, whether they are real or imaginary. What traits or qualities do they exhibit? You probably already have some of these, while others could use some work. None of us is perfect, but we tend to underestimate our own talents and abilities, as well.

What do you find to be truly thrilling and exciting?

What do you do (or possibly wish you could or would do) that gets your blood pumping? Regardless of whether it fits in with other career and life goals, most of us need a good jolt of adrenaline now and again just to remember that we are alive. What activities or relationships in your life give you that feeling?

What do you think is really true about life, or the universe?

This is a terribly open-ended question, and it should be. By its very nature, truth never changes. Our understanding of it, however, is constantly growing and evolving. Finding that anchor for your beliefs is integral to developing faith, of course, but it also factors into your own values by giving you a sense of what you agree with and want to share with others.

What do you care about most in the world?

Note that "most" doesn't necessarily have to indicate something singular in a sense. It might be that, for you, your family and friends, a charitable cause, and college football are all high priorities. It might sound or seem a little funky to put them together, but the idea isn't to stick to convention, but to stay true to yourself. Go with your gut instincts.

What set of things would you most love to accomplish in your life, whether they have anything to do with your career or not?

This really speaks to two different topics: experiences and legacy. What do you still have left to do? And, just as importantly, what do you want to leave behind for others when you're done?

What kinds of regrets keep you up at night?

Although you certainly don't want to dwell on the negative, you can learn a lot from parts of your life that didn't turn out the way you wanted or expected them to. If you're holding on to some regrets, why not use them to help yourself build a meaningful life going forward?

What would you never do again if you had the choice?

As I hope I made clear earlier, *Seeking Your Center* isn't just about living out your fantasies or avoiding any kind of uncomfortable sensation. And so, when you're looking for the answers to this question, you should look past day-to-day annoyances like sitting in traffic or filing taxes, that we all deal with, and think about the bigger defining moments. It might be that you never want to disappoint a loved one again or fail to complete a major project. Think things through and try to find a feeling, experience, or sensation that you'd like to be done with. *What do you think is necessary for you to have a happy and fulfilling life?*

By now, some of the other questions have probably helped you to find the answer to this one. List anything that you think is essential for your long-term happiness, including the relationships that are most important to you, the activities that most excite you, and the qualities or purposes that seem to come to the front of your mind again and again.

As you begin to answer these questions, you'll probably find that a few interesting things begin to happen. For one thing, you might find that you have satisfying answers to some but not all of the questions. Or there are some you can answer instantly, while others would require hours of notes to even scratch the surface.

Also, you may quickly begin to sense that the answers you do have don't necessarily go together, or lead you toward any sort of big life direction. That's perfectly all right. In the same way that listing your favorite foods wouldn't necessarily help you create a good recipe, the point of this exercise isn't to find the perfect job or outline your "perfect day" – it's just about discovering what's important to you.

And finally, don't feel frustrated or disappointed if you move through these questions several times, at length, and still don't feel like you have satisfactory answers. Often, we've gone so long without thinking about our inner motivations that we've effectively hidden them from our own consciousness. It might take a little bit of time and effort to discover them again.

Working through a questionnaire isn't the only way to learn what you want to know about yourself, so let's look at some other ways you can study your own motivations and priorities.

Other Ways to Tap into Your Values

If the answers you found in the previous section don't seem specific, concrete, or true, there are other things you can try.

One of the first is to ask yourself whether you're holding on to notions or conventions that really belong to someone else. In other words, if you're answering the way you *think* you should, instead of the way you truly feel. It's not unusual to try to "fit in," even unconsciously, so look out for anything that doesn't seem to have a ring of truth to it.

Another option is to invest in personality testing, which is widely available online. You may have already undergone these kinds of assessments in the past for an employer, but our desires and motivations often change over time, meaning that the answers you get now might be different – or more meaningful – than they were before. These kinds of tests can remind you about aspects of yourself that you had forgotten or weren't even consciously aware of. It's hard to self-diagnose and self-analyze, so there can be real value here.

That's particularly important when you understand that many of our most important values and personality traits live on an unconscious level. Moreover, some of those might not be entirely positive (like a desire to dominate others or accumulate personal power for the wrong reasons).

Moreover, some of the values and tendencies we hold might actually be in conflict with one another. The resulting internal tug of war can be a huge stumbling block in your life. The best way to overcome it is simply to be aware of what's going on in your mind so you can be conscious of any traits you want to minimize or deemphasize. We all have parts of ourselves that we aren't particularly fond of; by gaining awareness of those traits, we take the first step toward mastering them.

Yet another method for discovering your values is simply talking to your associates and loved ones. As we all know, it can be easy to miss the obvious when you're too close to something. By bringing people who see and observe you every day into the equation, you might get a different perspective that's insightful. Sometimes we just don't know ourselves as well as our spouses, parents, and partners do.

A different way to approach the problem is to look at your own past actions and experiences. Once most of us get past our adolescent years, we discover that certain patterns and themes emerge in our life again and again. Some could be the result of pure coincidence, but most tell us something about the way we think, what we truly hold dear, and what we hope to achieve.

If you still don't have the answers, or want to keep exploring, consider brainstorming out loud. Spend a couple of hours with a good friend, or even a professional therapist, and just start talking. You'd be amazed at the kinds of discoveries we can make when we let our minds roam free on a problem or topic. Suddenly, the things we thought we didn't see, know, or understand come pouring out. And, if you're having trouble identifying your own values, this could be a valuable step to take.

An Example from My Own Life

However you approach the process of discovering your values, know that it might take a while... and certainly longer than most people would expect. I know this from firsthand experience, and because my values have changed from one time period to another.

Currently, I think that the most important qualities or ingredients of my life and career are: *spirituality*, *family*, *leadership*, *adventure*, and *loyalty*.

That might seem like a simple list, but it's one that accurately reflects all of the most important roles and visions I have for myself at present. They are things that get me out of bed in the morning, and make me feel content when I lay my head on my pillow at night.

What's more, they often help me identify what's wrong when I start to feel off-center. For instance, I tend to find that if I don't do something crazy and ill advised at least twice a year, I begin to get a little bit irritable and less effective in *all* the areas of my life.

Because I know that a sense of adventure is so important to me, I make a conscious effort to leave time for it on a regular basis. It isn't the biggest part of my life, and not my most important value, but it matters – without it I move away from my center and that loss of momentum carries through to my career and relationships. The same applies to my sense of family and spirituality. Even though they represent different parts of my life, I need them all working more or less in harmony to be at my best.

Defining Success on a Personal Level

One of the difficulties of working through self-assessment questions and defining values is that it can seem like you're on a search for something that's wrong or missing. That's not necessarily the case. Lots of successful people find that they are already moving toward their center, and that a lot of their identified values are in line with their personal and professional lives. Discovering what they really want or need, or just why they're doing the things that they're already doing, can be valuable in and of itself.

Conversely, you may start to feel like you need to make some bigger life changes and choices (something we'll address a bit more later in the book). That's perfectly all right, too. What we're shooting for isn't the definition of the perfect person, or even to turn you into something the rest of society will look up to and admire. Instead, what we are trying to create is the vision of *your personalized success*.

> **When your last breath comes, it isn't going to matter what anyone else thought about the way you should have lived your life, only whether you feel satisfied with it or not.**

Stop and think about that notion for a moment. It's a pretty profound realization, and it has guided my thinking through every chapter and topic of this book.

When you're at your center, you can feel satisfied with where you're going and what you've done. You've won at the game of life not because you've accumulated the most or accomplished a certain level of fame or notoriety, but because you've made yourself feel satisfied and worked to live as the best version of you that you could possibly be. As a byproduct, you will also have touched the lives of others who are connected to you as part of the human condition. You will have made a significant difference to your loved ones as well as yourself.

Additionally, you'll probably have been able to accomplish things you couldn't have dreamed of otherwise, and impacted the lives of dozens or hundreds of others. You'll have affected organizations and touched friends and loved ones in a way that will last the rest of *their* lives, too.

Most importantly, though, you'll have the sense of peace and contentment that can only accompany a life well lived. Even though you might have a seemingly endless supply of energy, you won't feel like you spent your days moving in a haze or giving half of your effort. That's the way I want you to feel and what *Seeking Your Center* is all about.

This chapter was all about helping you to find your values, which are the internal foundation that you're going to build the rest of your life on. Put together with the five tenets of *Seeking Your Center*, they create a formula for fulfillment and inner peace.

CHAPTER EIGHT

Obstacles to Reaching Your Center

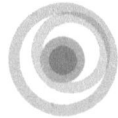

In the beginning of this book, I asserted that *all of us* are yearning for center, whether we know it or not. For most, the search isn't a formal process, but something that just comes with acquiring wisdom and planning ahead for the rest of our lives. But, they are still doing it nonetheless.

If that's the case, though, why aren't more of us actually *finding* our centers?

The most straightforward answer is that a lot of people don't know their center actually exists. Maybe they have experienced it, but didn't recognize it for what it was at the time. Or, they think of it as a feeling of exhilaration that is hard to duplicate or repeat on a continual basis. These are usually the thoughts of men and women who think of life as a chore to be endured, rather than a journey to be savored.

They don't believe there is anything out there beyond their day-to-day existence, so they don't consciously seek center at all. Nor do they frequently find it.

Another reason is that the mundane can become overwhelming. That is, a person's life can be so crammed with details, obligations, and urgent but unimportant matters that they just don't have the time to think about what more they could be feeling or doing.

> **Note that this isn't always entirely unintentional; some people would rather stay busy than confront the gaping hole they feel when they stop to think, so they stay involved in so many different activities or social groups that they simply 'don't have a moment to spare.'**

And that's just the way they like it.

Yet another reason is that some people are dealing with physical and mental hurdles that take up a lot of their conscious attention, or make deeper introspection all but impossible. Certain physical ailments and emotional scars can act like mud on a windshield, hiding everything that's behind them in a curtain of muck.

And finally, there are men and women who would like to live at or near their center, but simply don't know where to begin. Maybe the questions they are contemplating are new to them, or they haven't been able to find the answers they were looking for in books, seminars, or rituals they've tried in the past.

In this chapter, we are going to try to consider all the major obstacles to finding your center, so you can be aware of any that might be holding you back. Know from the outset, though, that all of these obstacles are deeply personal, and each of them can be overcome. Finding your center is largely a matter of discovering the strength that's within you and comes from your purpose, values, and faith. Once you are aware of them, and know how to move forward, you'll be equipped with all the tools you need to get past anything that's in your way.

Getting Past Skepticism

In New York State, lottery tickets used to be marketed with the slogan, "You can't win if you don't play." Even though the odds of finding your center are much better than winning millions, it's a useful notion for figuring out why most people never become centered.

> **When you fail to search for your center, you leave things entirely to chance. If you don't search, you can't find.**

We live in a world where skepticism runs high. If you make a big claim, you can bet that someone will be standing by to disbelieve it or knock it down, regardless of whether it's legitimate or not. That leaves lots of people afraid to search for a better life, or more purpose, because they think the idea is "too good to be true." Or, they think that centeredness is something that they can only achieve by turning their whole lives upside down.

If that sounds like you, it's time to let go of your skepticism and accept the fact that it might be your own beliefs and attitudes that are holding you back. We were all built and designed to fulfill our ultimate purpose, whatever that might be. If you can't trust in that idea, though, you will never enjoy the mental and spiritual benefits that are waiting for you.

Even though I might be calling it by a different name, the concept of center is virtually as old as mankind itself. People have always wanted to live fulfilling lives, to be excited and content all at the same time. In fact, it's probably a yearning you have within yourself right now, which is what led you to pick up a copy of this book (or led someone else to get a copy for you). I wholeheartedly believe the approach I'm giving you is going to make it easier for you to find your center, but that only works if you're willing to believe in it in the first place.

In the introduction, I asked you to consider moments in your life when you felt like you were at your center, even if you didn't think about it in those terms. Go back to those experiences, or think about the men and women we described earlier on. Understand that you can enjoy the achievement and inner peace that they have. You can make your life more enjoyable, dynamic, and purposeful all at the same time.

If you can put your skepticism aside and hold on to that one grain of trust (or hope), that should be enough to help you get started. And once you begin the process of seeking your center, the changes you will see in yourself and your vision of the future are going to carry you the rest of the way.

Relationships and Environmental Influences

Some psychologists theorize that each of us really just amounts to the sum personality of the dozen or so people we spend most of our time with. While I think that takes things a little bit too far, it's hard to argue with the idea that we are all influenced by our relationships, and especially our closest ones.

As you'd probably expect, that can be a really good thing or a really bad one.

> **If you surround yourself with people who are supportive – and who are trying to stay motivated and live lives that are in line with their own values – it's going to feel natural for you to do the same. And, if you're surrounded by others who are constantly negative, or make you feel worse about yourself, then you can't be surprised when those impressions rub off on you, either.**

There's really nothing unexpected about the way this happens. If you were to spend several hours a day listening to the same radio station, it wouldn't take long before you recognized all of their most popular songs. What's more, you would know the frequent advertisements by heart and get acquainted with the styles and mannerisms of each DJ.

Most of us spend far more time with our closest family and friends than we do listening to our radios, and the "songs" we hear – or in this case, the underlying messages – are repeated a lot more often. And you can be sure we put a lot more stock in the advice we get from our closest friends than we ever do the different ads and clips that come over the airwaves.

With that in mind, one obvious way to help yourself find center is to think about the ideas and notions you're actually getting from people you are choosing to spend your time with. Decide whether it's helpful support, negative criticism, or something in between. In some cases, the smartest thing to do might be to work on the way you and those closest to you communicate with one another; other times, it might be necessary to actually find some new friends and replace destructive relationships with more positive ones.

Even men and women who are close to their centers can find that they have friendships and partnerships with people that they possibly shouldn't. Sometimes we hang on to others out of sheer habit; other times they are old friends who were associated with other important periods in our lives.

We'll explore the best ways to think about those relationships, and particularly your closest relationships, later in the book when we help you contemplate major changes. For now, though, it's best to simply be aware of the inputs that you're getting from others. Do you feel like your interactions with your spouse, family members, and closest work associates are helping you move toward your center, or pulling you away from it?

Physical Pain, Stress, and Fatigue

Although finding your center is more a mental and spiritual exercise than it is a physical one, your physical state and well-being can still influence the process. After all, it has been accepted in almost every culture for thousands of years that the mind, body, and spirit are inseparable.

In a general sense, this means that it's difficult to concentrate on things like spirituality, self-awareness, and your true purpose when you're in the midst of physical pain. On the other side of the coin, it also means that it's easier to stay at your center emotionally when you feel good physically, if only because you are more energetic and your mind has fewer distractions.

Taking care of yourself physically also means you should take steps to manage chronic health problems or conditions that you feel might be holding you back. A lot of us have gotten pretty good at ignoring minor symptoms of bigger physical issues, but pretending they don't exist won't make them go away. Nor is it going to help us find balance in our lives. Being healthy and pain-free is its own reward, but it's also important if you want to find your center and reach your potential.

Although we don't often think of them as being in the same category of other physical problems or illnesses, it's worth pointing out that stress and fatigue can certainly stand in the way of finding your center. Left unchecked, either has the ability to harm us in a lot of ways that aren't always apparent on the surface. Not only can they lead to bigger, more severe health problems by lowering our immune response, but they have the potential to pull our awareness away from our own purpose and emotions.

> **In other words, stress and fatigue dull us to things that are going on around us, not to mention things that are happening *within* us. Being tired and stressed out affects the way you think about everything else in your life, making every day seem less sharp and less interesting – which is essentially the opposite of feeling centered.**

There are a lot of things you can do to manage stress and fatigue, beginning with getting more rest and living in a way that's consistent with your goals and values. Excessive strain or a sense of being tired all the time are often a clear sign that we've gotten our priorities out of order and that we need to make changes before we can get back on track. Of course, the process of finding your center is often stress-relieving in and of itself, so you may find that the farther you go on this journey, the less these types of chronic problems actually may bother you.

Stress and fatigue can eventually be overcome with major or minor lifestyle changes, but what about physical problems that *can't* be resolved? What if you have nagging injuries, a serious health problem, or even a terminal illness? Can you still find your center under those circumstances?

You absolutely can. The key is to feel as good as you can in any possible moment. From headaches and indigestion to injury and disease, physical problems are generally only as debilitating as we allow them to be. Although you never want to have to learn to live with an unnecessary ache or pain, humans have a surprising resiliency when it comes to adjustment. Very few people find that they can't focus as the result of a physical problem, especially once they have taken available steps to mitigate the issue.

In cases of very serious illness, a physical ailment can actually make it easier to find your center. That's because extreme conditions, such as a life-threatening disease, tend to melt away the distractions most of us hold on to. They provide a clarity of thought and purpose that most people never experience, which can make it easier to recognize your values, find your faith, and live near your center.

Each of us should be doing all that we can to clear our minds and physical barriers to finding our center, but that isn't the same as saying that we are always going to be in perfect health all the time. Instead, it means we're not allowing minor problems with our physical bodies to dictate our thinking or dominate our consciousness any more than necessary.

Negative Thoughts and Emotional Pain

Negative emotions like greed, jealousy, and excessive pride or lust are all part of life. And yet, people who are living near their center experience them only briefly, and are able to shrug them off, while those who are far from center feel consumed by them.

> **Even though these thoughts might be part of the human condition, the problem with negative emotions is that they are antithetical to our values.**

Greed, for example, can destroy your sense of financial harmony. Jealousy can do the same, or take away comfort you feel with your inner circle. Lust can cause you to lose your self-integrity and live in a way that's not in line with your values, and so on.

The challenge, though, is that these feelings often linger beneath the surface of our consciousness. In order to remove them (or at least not be dominated by them), we have to do two different things: first, to be aware of them in the first place, and second, to replace them with something better.

In the first sense, being more self-aware is an important part of finding your own center, and a good habit for anyone who wants to break bad habits. There are a number of ways to do this, and one of the best is to review your day at a few set intervals. All you have to do is jot down notes on what you have been doing, and what you have been feeling, every few hours. Within a week or so, you'll start to notice patterns emerging in your own actions and emotions. These can help you find your strengths and weaknesses, even if they aren't apparent.

Another way to accomplish the same thing is by spending more time with loved ones and spiritual advisors, asking them for an outside perspective. Often, they'll be able to decipher emotional signs and signals that you wouldn't be able to pick up on yourself.

And finally, in the same way that you practice your values, you can practice your emotions. Using daily testimonials and reminders, you can actually make yourself more grateful and cheerful (and in the process, minimize tendencies toward greed and anger, as an example). If you think back to the example of a radio that I gave you before, you'll see why this works – all you're doing is changing the message in your mind.

In the same way that stress, fatigue, and other physical problems can be debilitating in a hidden way, emotional injuries can be destructive and obscured at the same time. Of course, these come in many different flavors and varieties.

> **No one escapes life unscathed, and we all know that carrying 'baggage' is just part of life on Earth.**

If you're dealing with some sort of severe trauma or unresolved conflict, though, that's going to express itself in a lot of different ways – and distract you from finding your true purpose.

Just as it's up to someone with a health problem to address it through physical or medical therapy, emotional pain should be worked through with the assistance of counselors, therapists, and/or spiritual advisors. The route you take to resolve the issue isn't as important as taking the actual first step is. That's because, even if you aren't aware of any interference in your personal or professional life, unresolved feelings can affect you in ways that you don't even notice or expect. These emotions are like a heavy, unseen backpack hanging from your shoulders. You might not notice them much at first, but eventually they'll start to wear you down and slow your progress in life.

There is a segment of the population, and especially among high achievers, that believes that a bit of pain is a good thing. This belief is built upon the idea that our failures and humiliations make us stronger and drive us to reach heights that we wouldn't have without the extra motivation. Judging from my own experiences, there is some truth to this idea. Some people are undoubtedly driven to succeed just to prove others (or themselves) wrong.

However, even though drawing on failure might help you reach a certain level of material success, making some kind of pain or disappointment the centerpiece of your motivation ultimately poisons those triumphs and limits your happiness. Try to learn from your history; don't dwell on it to the point that it becomes something that defines you.

Dealing with Unrealized Expectations

Surprisingly enough, a great deal of the emotional pain that a lot of us carry around with us is self-inflicted. To be sure, we don't mean to damage our own moods and confidence, but we go ahead and do it anyway in the form of unrealized expectations.

These expectations may begin with ideas or aspirations planted in our minds by teachers and parents. By reinforcing those notions again and again, we internalize them. "You *could* be a star athlete" becomes "you *need* to be a star athlete," or "follow my example" turns into "you need to be more successful than your father was." Often, these expectations are never actually stated or explicitly agreed to by anyone, yet they feel like unresolved obligations all the same.

> **This matters a great deal because unresolved expectations *always* lead to conflict.**

To see why this is the case, consider what happens when two people get married. Even if they never speak it out loud, both parties are going to come into the relationship and arrangement with expectations in mind. Perhaps the husband thinks that the wife should be able to cook and clean, or the wife feels that the husband ought to earn a good living and stay home most nights of the week.

The minute that one of these partners fails to meet those expectations – again, expectations that might not have ever been expressed or agreed upon – resentment and conflict are going to be part of the equation. Arguments are likely going to ensue, and one or both spouses are going to begin to "act out" because their expectations haven't been met.

The obvious solution is for both parties to get together and *agree* on the expectations they have set for each other, which is exactly what a lot of relationship counselors will do at this point. However, if the expectations you are carrying around are entirely internal, or have to do with people who aren't in your life anymore, then these issues can be more difficult to resolve.

In those cases, it's up to you to decide what's important as you move forward, and to let go of obligations or expectations that no longer make sense in the direction you're hoping to take.

Letting Go

You've probably noticed that a common theme among each of these emotional issues, regardless of whether you think of them as injuries, negative thinking habits, or unmet expectations, is that eventually you have to find a way to simply *let go*.

This is simple, time-tested, and entirely appropriate advice. But that doesn't mean it's easy, or that letting go of an old idea or resentment is going to be as simple as brushing a piece of lint off your shoulder. The fact of the matter is that past insults, defeats, and problems tend to linger on and on, far after the time when they've actually been useful or relevant. In many cases, the people and situations in question are no longer part of our lives... but that doesn't stop us from dwelling on them.

The trick to letting go is usually to take some kind of action. For example, if you're holding a grudge against a former friend or a distant relative, now might be a great time to speak with them on the phone, or even meet for a cup of coffee. Explain that you feel like you've been holding on to an unnecessary piece of anger or annoyance and that you think it's time to move past it. Sometimes, this might lead to the renewal of an old friendship. Other times, the person either won't remember the feud or will still refuse to forgive you. No matter what, though, you're moving toward closure, and that might make you feel better.

Things become more difficult when the damage has been more severe, of course, or when the person in question isn't in your life anymore (or is perhaps impossible to reach). Still, there is some action you can probably take, even if it's simply writing a letter that you never intend to send. Just take the action and let it go. Or if you can't do that, at least find a mental health professional or spiritual advisor who can help you start moving on from the trauma. Even if the healing doesn't come all at once, you'll feel less bothered and preoccupied by expressing the thoughts rather than holding them in.

This kind of forgiveness also happens to be a two-way street. That is, although you are likely more aware of people who have wronged you or a shred of anger that you're holding on to, it's likely there are others that you have wronged, too. Now is the time to start making apologies and removing the weight from your chest. There isn't any guarantee that you'll be able to track down everyone you want to or that they'll necessarily forgive you for whatever you've done wrong. But, by taking this step, you can help yourself to move back toward your center by getting rid of old bits of emotional baggage that are weighing you down and clouding your thinking.

Momentum and Inertia

To this point, I've made quite a point of telling you that reaching your center involves a willingness to change and accept new things. But, those need to be the right kinds of changes, made for the right reasons, and executed in a way that doesn't leave you feeling upside down.

This is important because human beings aren't built to turn their lives on a dime. Every year, men and women who are looking for answers try all kinds of unconventional solutions. Some put their trust in New Age philosophies and crystals, or meditation sessions in sweat lodge retreats held out in the middle of the desert. In each case, their hearts are in the right place, but more often than not, these kinds of drastic measures lead to dramatic lifestyle changes that aren't well thought out and prove impossible to maintain.

To put things more bluntly, if you quit your job, change your profession, and file for divorce in the span of a week, all because you found a "new" philosophy, you're probably going to find yourself moving away from your center, rather than toward it. There are gurus who will be happy to tell you in under an hour how to spend the rest of your life if you pay them, but that's really the equivalent of putting your life savings on a roulette wheel in Las Vegas.

Finding your center is a matter of choosing a direction, of course, but it's also about avoiding quick impulses and overcoming inertia. You need to build momentum steadily, and avoid doing what you've always done even though it might be a little bit easier or more convenient.

When it comes down to it, that's probably the most important thing to remember about *all* the obstacles to centeredness. Most of them involve holding on to things we shouldn't in one form or another. The longer you stay at it, and the more sure you feel in your purpose, the easier it's going to be to break away from whatever defined your life in the past and start becoming the kind of person you always knew you wanted to be.

SEARCHING FOR CENTER

- *What do you think are your biggest obstacles to reaching your center right now?*

- *How is your own skepticism preventing you from finding inner peace?*

- *What emotional baggage are you clinging to that is preventing you from reaching center?*

CHAPTER NINE

Resources for Seeking Center

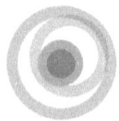

*Y*our center might be a personal concept, and finding it may be largely a matter of self-discovery, but that doesn't mean others can't help you on your journey. In the same way that your inner circle is incredibly important to keeping you at your center, there are others who can guide you in an ongoing way toward the values and principles that matter most to you.

For the sake of this chapter and discussion, I'm going to refer to the four groups of people who can help you on your journey as "resources." Realize, though, that these are just different types of relationships that we have with others. When it comes to finding your center, they are very specific types of interactions you want to develop with others who can guide you on your path because of the unique knowledge or insight they have. Additionally, it could be that you will also fulfill these roles at one time or another for someone else.

What matters most right now, however, is that you understand who these people are, and why the relationships are so important to reaching your center. Let's start by identifying the four main categories that they fall into:

☐ Comforter   ☐ Spiritual Advisor
☐ Counselor   ☐ Mentor

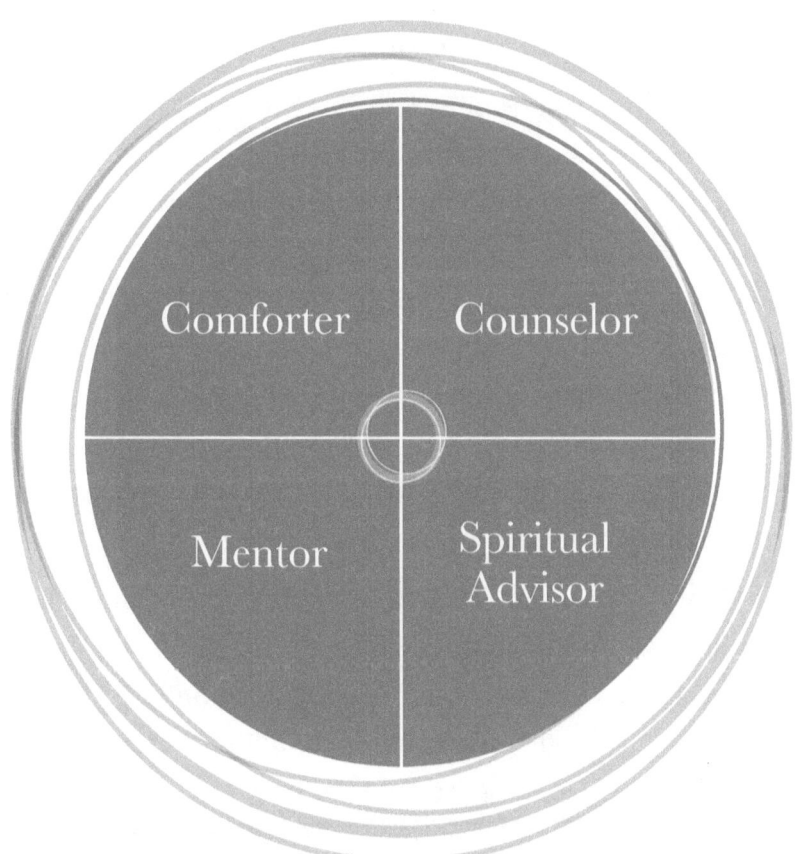

Comforter

A comforter is someone in your life who is as close to you as any other human can be. They are usually a spouse/partner, a best friend, or a very close relative.

A good rule of thumb is to think about the first person you'd want to call the moment you receive a piece of really good or bad news. A comforter knows your deepest thoughts, secrets, and motivations. They aren't just the person you confide in, but someone you trust to support you at every turn. You might often get the feeling they "know you better than you know yourself."

In fact, that can be one of the biggest benefits of having a person who fills the comforter role for you. Sometimes, we get so turned around in life that it's hard to remember what we really want, or which values and ideas matter most to us. In essence, things can get so hectic and confused we lose track of who we really are. In that situation, your comforter can help remind you of your own thoughts and impressions. They can hold a mirror up to your ideas and help you discover the truth when it comes to things like your true purpose or hidden values.

This is true even when the feedback isn't altogether positive. As I've mentioned a few times, none of us is perfect. If we were, we wouldn't struggle to find and live at our centers in the first place. Often, it falls to the comforters in our lives to help us figure out where we might be coming up short or failing to meet our own expectations. Part of their role is to ensure that we really know ourselves, which includes the good *and* the bad.

> **Your comforter can also be a tremendous source of love and support. No matter how strong we are in our careers or what we've accomplished in our personal lives, we all need someone who is 'in our corner' from time to time.**

We need to have those relationships we know we can fall back on, and to have someone who is guaranteed to love us, encourage us, and push us forward when things aren't going our way.

Remember, though, that your comforter doesn't just exist to assist you. If your relationship with this person is going to remain healthy, there needs to be a give-and-take. Part of that is being a comforter for them yourself; another part is taking responsibility for that bond and nurturing the relationship on an ongoing basis. In other words, you don't just turn to this person when you need something, but you make them a major priority in your life.

Nearly everyone who's reading this book either has a comforter already or would like to find one. Just remember this person doesn't necessarily have to be involved with you romantically; they just have to care about you and share a deep, personal connection with you.

In some ways, the comforter is the easiest person on my list to find, as there aren't any particular experience or qualification needs. And yet, most of us spend the better part of our lives looking for comforters. Without this kind of relationship in your life, a certain degree of loneliness is inevitable. So, if you don't already have a comforter you can count on and turn to, make finding this kind of relationship a big priority. And if you do already have someone you love, trust, and connect with, make sure to take care of that relationship and realize that it probably means more to your well-being than you know.

In my own life, my wife, Amy, serves as the ultimate comforter for me. When things aren't going my way, the expectations I've set for myself aren't being met, or I just seem to meet with personal or professional setbacks, she's the first person I turn to. That's more than just companionship or support; my relationship with her is like a foundation or rock that lets me continue living near my center more frequently.

Having a comforter doesn't just mean you spread your sorrows and troubles to another person, either. Every joy in my life is enhanced when I'm able to share my triumphs with her or when she has something great happen and shares it with me. Your comforter doesn't have to be a spouse or even a romantic partner. Having someone that you turn to and share your life with, though, makes the bad times more bearable, and good ones come around a lot more often.

Counselor

Generally speaking, when someone suggests that you "seek professional help," it isn't meant in a complimentary way. When it comes to finding your center, though, it's not a bad idea. After all, professionals are professionals for a reason; often, they can help us get into touch with our own goals, habits, and ideas in a way that others who are closer to us can't.

There are a number of people who could fit the "counselor" role for you in your personal and professional life. Most will fall into the category of business coaches, executive development professionals, or even therapists or psychologists. Their role in your journey is clear: to provide a trained, subjective frame of reference to help you discover what you really want and need in your life, or what could be holding you back from living near your center more often.

Throughout this book, I have made a point of highlighting the notion that reaching your center is largely a matter of self-discovery. As much as you need to know what goes into your center, it's just as important to recognize what it feels like to you, and how your journey might differ from someone else's. Having the right counselor – or team of counselors – around you can make that a bit more accessible. They generally have training and experience that allow them to ask questions you might not have thought of on your own, or help you make connections that might have remained hidden without their guidance.

Occasionally, I meet with men and women who have a reluctance to meet with a professional counselor or advisor of any kind. In some cases, they might be afraid of the investment of time or money needed to get this kind of help. I can certainly relate to that, but I still think it's worth a few of your dollars and a little bit of time, especially as you work through the kinds of issues outlined in the last chapter.

On the one hand, a counselor might be able to expedite the process or make certain things more clear to you. And on the other, they can often assist you with clearing up the kinds of doubts, resentments, and expectations so many people are holding on to. Those kinds of negative thoughts, memories, and impressions can keep you from your center and stop you from realizing your full potential. Isn't it worth a little something extra to keep your life moving in a positive direction?

Another reason people put off professional help from counselors is because they think they'll just hear things they already know. It's true that some of the advice or insight you get from a counselor might overlap with what you would hear from a comforter, mentor, or spiritual advisor. Still, because they fulfill different roles in our lives, they can offer the advice in a different way. And, because of their unique training and background, we might be more apt to actually pay attention to what they're telling us.

Yet a third reason people tend to avoid seeking out the counselors they need is because they realize they have gaps in their lives, but don't want them exposed or addressed. For some, the fear of having others know about their weaknesses and insecurities can be overwhelming. That can lead them to behaviors that are damaging to themselves and their relationships. Even worse, they may have faults they don't want to fix – in other words, they have vices or habits they are attached to. When we begin to enjoy our flaws too much, it's hard to ever move on from them.

Throughout my career I have gotten guidance and assistance from executive coaches who have made the path to professional success easier in a number of different ways. By analyzing my strengths and weaknesses, and helping me to improve the skill sets critical to my position, they've helped me go a lot farther than I ever would have on my own.

There were certainly monetary costs involved, but in my own experience, working with good counselors has been well worth the money in the long run. That's because I haven't just earned more as a result of their input, but have had doors and opportunities opened to me that I might not have discovered without their help.

I can't guarantee the same results for you, but virtually everyone I know who has worked with the right counselors has come out of it richer in both obvious and unexpected ways.

> **Counselors are important to you in your life because they have unique training and experience they can use to show you ideas, patterns, and even inspirations that might be difficult for you to express consciously or openly.**

You can't find your center until you truly know yourself and how to create change in your life. Doesn't it make sense to have experts who can help lead you on the right path?

Spiritual Advisor

In this context, the term "spiritual advisor" is important to define, if only because we haven't been talking about spirituality in a way that most people think of it or understand it. Just as spirituality in this book refers to the belief in *something* greater than yourself, your spiritual advisor should be someone who shares your core beliefs and can have in-depth discussions with you about them.

Naturally, this role could be filled by a priest, rabbi, or similar religious figure. However, even if you don't subscribe to any organized belief system, you can still have a spiritual advisor whom you talk to regularly. All that matters is that you can meet with them and expect consistent opinions, a bit of feedback, and a healthy give-and-take when it comes to discussing important matters of ethics and values. It helps if you have someone who has more of a spiritual background, or a broader set of experiences with a certain belief system (or different belief systems), than you do. In other words, you want to find a spiritual advisor who has pondered the kinds of questions you're having before and can at least offer some guidance toward answers that are in line with your beliefs.

The spiritual advisor is important to your center simply because your spirituality and faith are so central to the concept. Without a strong sense of spirit, it's easy to lose perspective, not to mention sight of your overall goals and values. But, as we'll discuss, life doesn't always cooperate and make it easy for you to stay at or near your center, spiritually or otherwise.

> **When the inevitable turmoil throws you off balance, your spiritual advisor is an important resource – a 'rock' who can keep you grounded in your faith, whatever that faith looks like.**

Although you could theoretically turn to your spiritual advisor as needed at different points in your life, you'll have an easier time staying in your center if you have someone you can meet with regularly. That's partly because you want your spiritual advisor to know a bit about you and your situation, and not just a belief system in general. It's also important, however, because your spiritual advisor can be an important link to your community at large, and especially other members of your "inner circle." Most of us form stronger relationships through spiritual beliefs than we can without them, even if we don't attend religious services. So, having a spiritual advisor that we meet with on a fairly predictable basis can be a good way to keep ourselves grounded.

To really get the benefit from having a spiritual advisor, you want more than just a one-way interaction.

I try to meet regularly with mine, for example, over the occasional breakfast or a cup of coffee. While this type of interaction might not be as formal, it allows us to have a direct dialogue. I can raise issues or questions that are on my mind, and my spiritual advisor can answer or bring up his own topics, as well.

Although it's low key, this has huge benefits for me. Like anyone, I go through periods where my belief systems and connection to my beliefs are challenged. Having someone to give me some positive and reinforcing feedback helps me hold on to my faith and stay centered no matter how chaotic the outside world seems.

Mentor

If I had to guess, I would say there have been hundreds upon hundreds of different books written about the power and value of mentor/protégé relationships. And yet, a great number of people – even among the most successful – don't have a mentor they can turn to when personal or professional questions come up.

In a basic sense, the value of a mentor is very easy to understand: They should be a person who has been in your shoes in the past and lived to tell the tale. They have an understanding of who you are, what you want to accomplish, and what kinds of steps and challenges lie in front of you. They've been down the road before, as the saying goes, and know not only where it leads, but which wrong turns you have to look out for.

For that reason, it helps if your mentor is more experienced and more successful than you are. Often, mentors tend to be older, but that's not necessarily a prerequisite for finding someone who can help you.

There are a lot of reasons to find a good mentor, especially when it comes to the development of your career. For those who are seeking center, however, mentors have special value because they can offer advice and perspective in a way that counselors usually cannot. While both have their place, the mentor is usually more personal, knowing both you and your career path in a more intimate way. And, because their qualifications are based on life experience instead of just degrees and training, they can give you guidance that is a bit more practical and seasoned than counselors sometimes can.

The best mentors also add a bit of patience and a long-term view to our thinking. Very frequently in life, the problems we face feel urgent and overwhelming. To a mentor who has been through the same issues in the past, though, they are often less severe than imagined. In fact, your mentor might be able to show you how simply waiting an issue out, or making small corrections to your course, can resolve things more quickly than you might imagine.

In other words, a good mentor keeps you near your center by helping you discover your purpose and avoid overreactions that pull you away from your center. They teach you not to put too much stock into short-term distractions that don't really matter so that you can keep your focus where it belongs. And, of course, they can set a wonderful example of the traits that we talked about earlier in this book, like kindness, humility, and a charitable mindset.

Early in my career, I came upon a professional choice that amounted to a fork in the road. There was an opportunity that held a lot of potential, but I just wasn't sure whether I should take it or not.

On the one hand, the new position would come with a great title and a bigger paycheck. It was undeniably a "step up" in the corporate ladder. But it also meant a lot of upheaval in terms of moving my family (and the connections they had to *their* inner circles), changing my own lifestyle and work/life balance, and taking on a completely new professional direction.

I was excited and paralyzed at the same time. Luckily, I had a mentor to turn to. This person didn't just have the benefit of many years of experience, but also knew me in a personal way and could see beyond the obvious issues.

The first thing he reminded me was that a situation that *looks* like a fork in the road is really just a decision point. When we get to these points, we have to make the best decisions we can given the life experience we have up until then and the information at hand. Once you realize that, you accept that it's possible to do your best without second-guessing yourself later. You'll never know the full outcome of a decision point when you're evaluating your options, and you can't ever go back and see how other decisions would have ultimately turned out in the long run, either. One decision point just leads to another. We should do our best with them one at a time without looking back too often.

After that, the specific advice he gave me included both short-term guidance and long-term perspective that I sorely needed. He was removed enough from the situation to provide an outside point of view, but had a history with me that stretched far beyond what any counselor or coach could learn in a few short sessions.

Not only did I make the decision that was best for my career and my family, but I was able to do it clearly and confidently because I had a mentor when I needed one most. Never discount the importance of having someone fill this role and the effect it can have on your professional life.

> **A great mentor uses their wisdom and experience to help you become a better version of yourself, which is almost always a good step to take if you want to reach your center and make the most of your life.**

Matching Roles to People

If you're not currently living near your center, you'll probably find there are at least one or two of these resources missing from your life. In fact, it could be that you don't have someone filling *any* of them, which makes it incredibly difficult to feel calm and connected on a consistent basis.

In that case, one of your first steps should be to start identifying men and women who can do these jobs in your life. Some might be personal friends and relatives; others might be business acquaintances or even professional advisors. Just remember, each one is important, and you shouldn't be afraid to make changes as needed. If you don't feel like your spiritual advisor is moving you toward your center, for example, look for someone else who can. If you aren't making enough time for the person who fills the role of a comforter, then reassess your priorities, and so on.

After that, you should remember that these roles are actually more important to your centeredness than individual relationships are. In other words, it matters that you have someone, not that you necessarily hold on to the person you have right now. This isn't to say that those who are closest to you don't have value; it's just a realistic way to deal with the change that life inevitably throws at all of us.

Whether you like it or not, people are going to come and go. You could move, take a new job, or find that you're no longer compatible with someone who was close to you in the past. Or, as unfortunate as it might be, a key figure in your life could pass away, change careers, or be forced to deal with personal issues that make it impossible for them to lend you the kind of guidance and support they've been able to offer in the past.

When these changes occur, they can feel disturbing, as if the earth has been pulled out from under you. But that doesn't mean you have to lose your center permanently. Instead, you should look for someone else who can fill the role that is now empty. Find a new mentor, seek out a new comforter, try a new spiritual advisor, or get to know a new counselor. It might be difficult, and the new relationship may not gel as quickly as you would like – it may not even work out at all. But, without the right resources in your life, you're always feeling a void.

We can't always hold on to the people that matter the most to us throughout our entire lives. What we can do, though, is stay committed to living near our center by making sure that we always have these four resources to count on at any particular time so they'll help us stay calm and content when things are going well, and move us back to our center when they aren't.

CHAPTER TEN

Moving Toward Your Center

*E*ven though this chapter is titled *Moving Toward Your Center*, the reality is that thinking about your values, finding your faith, and questioning which parts of your life are most (or least) satisfying are important steps. You've been on your way all along, and probably already feel a bit more centered and balanced as a result.

Nonetheless, this is where the magic starts to happen for a lot of people, because they take those values and beliefs they've identified as being the most important to their future and start to put them to good use. That's something that can impact the rest of your life for the better.

> **This is another good place to remind the reader that a big effect doesn't necessarily have to stem from a big change.**

Or, to put things a little more bluntly, know that I am not expecting you to sell off all of your possessions and move to a mountaintop, or to set aside three hours every day for meditation.

Because concepts like spirituality, values, and beliefs tend to get tied up with the idea of major life changes, a lot of people come into this process thinking they are going to be challenged to give up everything they know and love. That's just not going to work for most men and women, and wouldn't be the best course of action even if it did.

Just as I've contended all along, moving toward center might not be easy, but it doesn't have to be complicated. Let's look at four steps that are involved.

4 Steps to Finding Center

Once you've gone through the kind of self-discovery process that I have recommended already, there are four basic steps to finding and reaching your center:

- ✓ First, you have to have an awareness that your spiritual and emotional center exists, and that you're happier, more creative, and more productive when you're close to it.

- ✓ Second, you have to know what that centered feeling feels like, and which values, activities, and beliefs draw you closer to it, rather than push you away.

- ✓ Third, you create a clear vision for what your center will look and feel like once it has been achieved.

- ✓ And finally, you structure your life in such a way that you are constantly moving closer and closer toward those targets.

Most people struggle mightily with that fourth step. They want to be centered, but also have a lifetime of habits to overcome.

Those old habits and patterns don't have to represent an insurmountable struggle. If you've made it this far you already know two important things: whether or not you feel like you are at or close to your center already, and which values or tenets you need to prioritize to start getting closer if you aren't. The information and directions are right in front of you... it's time to look at some ways you can make the process of change easier.

Creating a Clear Vision for Your Center

Throughout this book, I've asked you to think about what your personal center is like. Chances are, even if you don't feel like you're living near your center, you've experienced happiness, exhilaration, and contentment at some point in the past.

Before we go any further, I want you to close your eyes for a moment and actually feel that sensation. What is it like? What have you been missing out on? What needs to change for you to return to that point?

You probably have some of the answers already, and this chapter is going to help move you even closer. However, until you have an actual sense of what being at your center is like – until you can feel it vividly within yourself – it's always going to remain a moving target that's difficult for you to reach.

That's the real value of having a clear vision for your centered life. Once you know what it looks like in a more specific sense, you'll have an easier time drawing your life toward it. If you think back to the metal detector I described early in this book, having a clear vision for your center is like adjusting your settings for gold, silver, or some other precious metal.

> **Until you know exactly what you're looking for, you're always going to have a hard time finding it.**

Start Thinking on a Longer Time Scale

Moving toward your center is partly about setting new habits, and just as much about letting go of old ones. You can make that easier to accomplish by simply adjusting the way you think. In particular, you want to start adopting a larger view of your life, and of the world around you.

A simple example of this can be found in the approach you take to health and fitness. Unhealthy people usually prefer instant gratification, looking for snacks and treats that make them feel better in the moment. Healthy people, on the other hand, choose foods based on how they want to look and feel later. They put off an instant sugar rush for the satisfaction of having more strength and energy when they most need it.

The same applies to most of our negative emotions, and the things that truly hold us back in life. Being angry, making impulsive decisions, ignoring long-term goals, or forgoing things like public service and charitable work often feel better, or at least easier, in the short term. But making progress on our most important goals in life, or enhancing parts of ourselves that we want to see grow and flourish, takes a bigger effort now while giving us the benefits we want later.

A lot of very successful people are in the habit of finding a vision they want to achieve in their professional lives, but fail to apply those same lessons and concepts to their personal goals. Regardless of what you have or haven't achieved up to this point, I'm asking you to put some time-honored principles to work when it comes to changing your attitudes, habits, and thought patterns. Any expert on psychology or performance can tell you that it isn't really possible to make lasting changes until you can envision them. So, don't pass up on creating a vision that's inspiring to you.

Replacing old habits with newer ones is never easy, but it's possible if we continually remind ourselves of what we are trying to achieve in the long run. Hold tight to your longer-term vision of the future, and of yourself, because that can give you the resolve you need to keep moving closer to your center over time. It *won't* be easy, but it *will* be worth it.

Tap into What Already Works

How often do you actually get to enjoy the activities that make you feel like you're at your center?

Those interests, regardless of whether or not they fit into your "life plan," can be incredibly important when it comes to moving toward your center over time. That's because they remind you of what it's like to be completely enthralled and consumed by an experience. That's something you should be seeking in all the parts of your life, which makes them valuable for learning, as well as just "letting off steam."

For instance, I've always had a love of aviation and one of my favorite hobbies is flying along in an ultralight-style aircraft. I try to make a point to take to the air a couple of times a year. Obviously, doing so isn't really helping my career, or my relationships with my loved ones, in any kind of strict sense. But even though my adventure value might not be as big a priority to me as my leadership or family values are, it's still there, and it still matters.

By taking the time to do something that excites me, I'm moving myself toward center with a sensory experience that I love. I'm also fulfilling a wish that makes it easier for me to enjoy my life, which in turn makes me a more effective leader and a more loving family member. And, I'm infusing that feeling of balance into my own mind.

You don't want to take this too far and start neglecting the other priorities in your life just to fit in every form of leisure you can dream up. But, if you have hobbies or activities that already make you feel centered, know that you aren't going to do yourself or anyone else much good by going without them. The parts of your life that already excite and engage you are important, and you can use them as a tool to keep pushing yourself in the right direction.

Make Space for What Is Important

As I hope you understand by now, doing things that feed into your most important values and priorities moves you toward center, and neglecting to do those things moves you farther and farther away. With that in mind, it's incumbent upon you to start making the time and mental energy for the things that matter.

In some cases, this might not be as hard as you think. Once you recognize that you *do* have a clear path forward, and one that can take you toward happiness and fulfillment, finding the focus and energy to make room in your life for new things could come naturally.

In other cases, it might be a bit harder because squeezing in something new can involve letting go of something old. These might be habits, activities, or even relationships that no longer work for you, or are holding you back from achieving the things that you truly desire deep down. More often than not, these turn out to be things we don't even love or enjoy anymore, but are simply afraid to let go of.

There isn't anything I can tell you that will make it easier. Human nature is such that we all like to stay where we're comfortable, even when we know it isn't the best thing for us. So, I invite you to ask yourself: What do you really want to be, and how do you really want to feel? The answers are probably evident already, and you may be procrastinating on a tough choice even when you know what to do.

> **There isn't any way around the fact that if you want to feel centered and fulfilled, you're going to have to make more room for things in some new parts of your life to grow. Once you've decided on a certain direction, commit to it and move forward without looking back.**

Making Big Changes

What do you do when you discover your most important values and beliefs aren't in line with the cornerstones you have built your life upon? In other words, what happens when you start to think your job, career path, or closest relationships (as examples) aren't helping you to move further toward your center?

My first piece of advice would be not to ignore these feelings. If you have the sense something is wrong now, it's only likely to become more exacerbated over time. At the same time, you don't want to make sudden, rash decisions, either.

For one thing, it could be you're just going through a rough patch with some aspect of your life. Things might not be as bad as they seem in the short term. In fact, it's a good idea to ask yourself whether, and how, circumstances have changed for you recently. A lot of times, what seems like a problem in your closest relationships or career, for example, simply stems from living very far from your center. Remember, all the different parts of your life are connected, and your happiness, contentment, and fulfillment in one area are going to naturally spill over to another. That's true in a positive sense, and a negative one as well.

You don't want to throw out the baby with the bathwater just because one part of your life is out of balance. Before you can make big changes, you have to be sure you're properly evaluating the situation at hand.

It could be the case that a little more work is needed – maybe you should be putting more effort into your job, or your relationships. Sometimes, doing the hard work so many of us want to avoid in the office, or at home, is all that's required to put things back on track. Staying the course and recommitting yourself can also be the smarter move on a lot of occasions. It goes without saying that there can be heavy, long-lasting legal and financial ramifications to turning your life upside down in an instant.

Supposing the problem isn't something that's going to be worked out without a major change taking place, however, then your next step might be to seek out advice. This could include feedback from a counselor, lawyer, or financial planner, of course, but you should also involve those trusted mentors and spiritual advisors we talked about earlier in the book. Get their insight and consider their advice. Ultimately, it's your choice on what direction you should take, but an outside perspective from someone who knows you can be invaluable when you're trying to untangle a particularly tough knot.

Another good idea is to revert back to those activities or experiences that you already know pull you toward your center. The goal isn't to get lost in them, but to find a place of calm and confidence where you can feel good about making decisions that may affect you, and your loved ones, for years or decades to come.

Finally, you have to decide which path to take forward. Just as I noted in the previous section, there really isn't a good way or template for making difficult decisions and carrying through with them. Sometimes the most important things in life are also the most difficult, and no chapter in any book is going to relieve that part of the human experience.

If you need to end a relationship, take your career in a new direction, or otherwise pursue a plan that's going to represent a U-turn from the path you were on before, it's probably going to cost you a lot of stress and sleepless nights. But it also might be the kind of decision you turn out to be incredibly grateful you made years from now. It's all up to you to create the kind of life that's going to put you on the path toward centeredness and fulfillment, and you shouldn't let a fear of change stand in your way.

A Word About Time and Change

As you have undoubtedly learned already in life, the things we want and need the most don't always happen the instant we expect them to. Change is hard, and forcing it often makes it slower and harder, not faster and easier.

This has two important effects that you should keep in mind. One is that you might need to manage yourself, and your own expectations, in a way that allows you to keep moving forward steadily one step at a time when you'd rather go barreling ahead. Hard as it might be, pacing yourself can make your move toward center a permanent process, rather than a one-time inspiration.

The other thing to be aware of is that even though the process of finding your center itself tends to bring peace, the slow change of progress that some people feel can be frustrating. This is where your faith – both in your beliefs and your desire to put your life on the right path – can come into play. Remind yourself of what you're trying to achieve, and why, and resolve to stick with it when things get tough. Believe these changes will occur in your life and that you will achieve your goal of moving toward your center. Have faith in yourself, and the entire process becomes much easier.

Ultimately, most people aren't going to find peace, gratitude, contentedness, and career direction overnight. But, by following the process I've outlined in *Seeking Your Center*, anyone can achieve all of those things and more. If you don't expect it to happen right away, you'll have the patience to find the right path and keep moving forward one step at a time.

SELF-DISCOVERY AND FINDING CENTER

> **Very early in this book, I warned you that finding your center is something you have to *do*, and not something you can simply read about and *have happen to you*.**

That's because this is a journey of self-discovery more than anything else. My center isn't the same as your center, and even though the tenets I shared earlier are universal across cultures and backgrounds, the specific answers and values attached to them are unique to an individual.

Just as two separate people can both be fit and in good physical condition even though they look very different, a pair of individuals who are both living near their center are going to share a lot of common traits, even though their respective lifestyles might look to be quite different from the outside. You could attribute this to differences in DNA, or the unique backgrounds and upbringings we all have. That certainly factors in, although I would also argue that each of us is built for a different purpose, so it wouldn't make sense for my values and mission to be exactly the same as yours.

When you recognize that, you understand the answers you're looking for can't be found just in this book. I can share with you the best ways to find them, but it's up to you to actually discover them and make them real.

Remember that seeking center is an intentional act. You are personally responsible for beginning and staying on the journey, and for finding the peace that is waiting for you.

CONCLUSION

Living Near Your Center

There is an old story that goes something like this:

A man seeks out a well-known monk and asks him how he was able to reach enlightenment. The monk thinks about it for a moment, and replies that he spent his days "chopping wood and carrying water." Surprised, the man then asks the monk how he lives *after* finding enlightenment. The monk smiles and replies, "Chopping wood and carrying water."

> **If that sounds like fortune-cookie wisdom, you're missing the point – finding your center isn't only about having experiences that are exhilarating and pulse-quickening. It's more about living every day to the fullest and feeling like you're slowly becoming the person that you were born to be, completing whatever mission you were put on this earth to finish. It's about the journey and not the destination.**

To be sure, finding your center more often will add excitement to your life. But you could get that same benefit from taking up rock climbing or skydiving. What we want isn't just to feel alive for a few fleeting moments, but to have a purpose that makes us feel more alive and engaged more of the time. And, to remember that everything in our lives is temporary and in constant motion. Your center is a moving target, so it's not going to live in the same place for very long.

How to Keep Moving Toward Center in a Sea of Change

We're now dealing with more change than ever. The fact of the matter is that simply keeping up with the details of your life can be difficult and exhausting. On the surface, that might make it seem harder to keep moving toward your center from one day to the next.

Although that might be partially true, I feel that it's akin to looking at things backward. Constant change is a reason to find your center, not avoid it. The closer you are to it, the more rooted you feel in your beliefs and values, regardless of what kinds of things are happening externally and outside your control.

One way to do that is to break out of your normal routines from time to time. It's a sad fact that many of us, Americans in particular, don't take the small amounts of vacation time afforded to us. Although the temptation to "get more done" can lull us into thinking we should stay at the office, it's usually the opposite that's true: The more space we make to get away, the more physically, mentally, and spiritually focused we become.

It doesn't take three weeks on a tropical beach to get back in touch with your goals, values, and beliefs. A change of scenery that lasts for just a couple of days can often do the trick, especially if you remove the normal distractions that come with work, constant interruptions, and the kinds of pressing problems that are urgent but not important.

Physical exercise can give you another way to keep your body and mind centered on a daily basis. As I've already mentioned, keeping fit is a habit worth holding on to in and of itself. Specific activities like yoga, meditation, or the martial arts can multiply the benefits you get from fitness because they force you to sharpen muscles *and* your concentration all at once. In that way, they provide a short "vacation" for your mind when it isn't consciously dwelling on the small aggravations and stressors that we all deal with.

Additionally, these types of activities help to lower your stress level, improve your self-confidence, and enhance your creativity. Because they can actually take you to center momentarily, they often become the kinds of hobbies you want in your life to stay close to your center.

Finally, you can always use basic psychology to your benefit and create daily reminders, habits, and affirmations that make you feel more centered in your life. The more personal they are, and the more touched or motivated you feel by them, the more effective they'll be in helping you to stay grounded from one day to the next.

Being Thrown from Your Center

Using the tools you have learned in this book, it should be possible for you to feel like you are close to your center more often. However, no one stays at their center continuously, if only because life tends to throw unforeseen obstacles in our direction, and some of them so large that no amount of self-exploration is going to resolve the problem.

Huge, life-changing events like divorce, bankruptcy, the loss of a business, the death of a loved one, or severe health problems can all leave you with more questions than answers, and feeling like you have been permanently removed from your center. In fact, in the midst of these kinds of events and emotions, you might feel as if your center is an illusion, and that you're going to be in a permanent state of grief or disarray for the rest of your life.

There aren't any words I can write that will take away the pain and sting associated with these kinds of traumas. Every life entails some sort of loss, but that doesn't make it hurt any less. What I can tell you, though, is that there isn't anything that can happen to you that can stop you from reaching toward your center. It certainly won't happen right away, but you can come back to the ideas, principles, and tenets you have learned to put the pieces back in place for a healthy, exciting, and fulfilling life.

Of course, the first step when you're facing a major loss or traumatic event is to simply give yourself the time you need to recover. No matter what you do or try, some emotions simply have to be processed and worked through; trying to "force" your way forward isn't going to help.

After a while, though, when you find you can contemplate your life and the future again, stop to think about which parts of your life in particular feel out of center now. Thankfully, very few of us experience the kinds of traumas that take away everything, from our inner circle to our financial harmony and spiritual awareness. If nothing else, we should have our faith to fall back on. By figuring out what we still have, we can begin the process of building our lives back up and reaching toward our center once again. It might not be quick, and it certainly won't be easy, but it's better than giving up and living without any kind of direction or inner peace.

In fact, that also brings us to another point: When you're living near your center, you are naturally more prepared for the kinds of jolts and shocks that life is going to throw your way. As I said, there is still likely to be pain, confusion, and even anger or grief. But, when you have the tenets and relationships you need in place, you are better equipped to withstand life-altering challenges, if only because you have faith, purpose, and the right kinds of people to fall back on.

I wish I could offer you a life that's free from pain and struggle, but that's not what finding your center is about. Instead, it's about being able to deal with anything life throws your way, and then knowing how to get back to a place where you feel energized and fulfilled once the initial shock is over.

Seeking Center Is About the Journey

As you might have guessed well in advance of this point, most people never reach an instant epiphany when it comes to finding their center. There isn't a lightning bolt of bright light, indescribable music, or an infinite moment where everything suddenly makes sense. Certainly, there *can* be moments that are like that, but I don't know of anyone who spends their day-to-day existence in that state... and if you think you know someone who does, there's a good chance they're trying to sell you something a lot more expensive than a book.

I've said all along that reaching center is a journey, rather than a finite destination. That's not necessarily bad news, though, even if you wish you could find instant gratification.

> **That's because simply looking for your center automatically pulls you closer to it, raising your awareness of your dreams and intentions one step at a time.**

When you begin to put the principles in this book to work, you start to gain confidence and improve your outlook. It's the kind of difference you can feel deep down inside.

Remember, most or all of us are feeling a draw toward center on one level or another. None of us wants to just survive – we all want to feel engaged, excited, and content with the knowledge that we are making a real difference in the lives of others and in the world around us. And, we want to feel like our best selves are coming forward each and every day.

Hopefully, you've followed along closely up to this point, and feel more centered as a result. Or, you at least have the sense that you could reach your center if you make some important changes in your life. That's a good first step.

Staying Aware of Your Center

Oddly enough, one of the easiest and most predictable ways to move from centered to off-center and out of balance is to stop making a conscious effort. Just as you have to work at your marriage, or your career, you should make a point of "auditing" yourself once in a while to figure out whether you're really living near your center on a regular basis. Are you truly feeling your purpose, and trusting in your faith? Or conversely, do you find yourself being bogged down by daily struggles and losing sight of the big picture? Do you feel calm and confident?

It's amazing how little it really takes to distract us from our most important purposes if we aren't paying close attention to them. You might think that, after going through the process of reflection and realignment outlined in this book, you would never be taken away from your center again. That might be true for some people, but for others small stressors and distractions creep in, chipping away at everything they've learned until they suddenly discover they are back to where they started.

To understand how this happens, just look back to an analogy I've already drawn on a couple of times: dieting and health. Lots of us develop bad eating and exercise habits throughout our adult lives. Then, in the midst of a major wake-up call (like a heart attack, for example), we decide to make some sudden and important changes. We know that, for a lot of different reasons, these changes matter a great deal. In fact, if we don't make them, we could pass away and fail to provide for our loved ones. And yet, all of those great intentions often fade away into the background as old habits resume. It isn't that we don't want to keep the changes we've made, but just that it's so much easier to fall back into old habits because it's difficult to maintain our focus 24 hours a day.

Luckily, living near your center doesn't usually have to involve making major changes all the time.

> **Instead, we simply have to exercise awareness and desire – we have to be aware that our center exists, and have the desire to keep moving toward it, no matter how hard life pushes in the other direction.**

Reminders, Prompts, and Habits

One way to counteract this emotional and spiritual entropy, and to stop life from pulling us away from our center, is to continually reinforce our awareness through daily habits and reminders. Going back to our previous example, someone who wants to alter their diet can post things like inspirational photos or quotes that help them keep their commitment to healthier eating in the front of their minds. The same goes for the tenets of center that we discussed earlier. By remaining focused on those, even using basic means like Post-it notes and other mental cues, we can keep our attention on the things that actually matter to us in the long term, rather than being pulled off track by every distraction that comes along.

Another good idea is to make room in your life for activities that are centering to you. These could include adventure trips, quiet time with your loved ones, or sessions with counselors that help you refine your purpose. They can also include those activities like yoga, martial arts, or spiritual services that hone our awareness and make it easier for us to focus on our daily lives. Trying any of these might require a little bit of effort and an open mind in the beginning, but eventually they become the sorts of habits that we find relaxing and renewing. As an added benefit, they tend to require very little in the way of time and monetary commitments, so they are easy to incorporate in your life.

You can also remain closer to your center by surrounding yourself with other people who are living near their centers, too. This works for a few different reasons. First, being around those who are stable, positive, and ambitious – as centered people tend to be – has the byproduct of drawing out those qualities in yourself, too. Next, the more people you know who are living near their center, the easier it is to find others to fill the comforter, spiritual advisor, mentor, and counselor roles that are so important. And finally, centered people can help you maintain the right perspective, professionally, spiritually, and otherwise, when difficult challenges or life conditions arise.

And finally, you'll want to be sure you make time to get away once a while, even if it's just for a day or two. Writers, artists, philosophers, and great thinkers have known for centuries that a change of scenery and perspective is often the easiest way to open up your mind and see your current situation in a new light. Even if you feel like you're very near your center, it's not a bad idea to take a break occasionally and reflect back on things. You may find that, as comfortable as you are, it's time for a new set of challenges. You might even take the time to run back through the exercises in this book. Reviewing them shouldn't take you as long as it did the first time, but you could be surprised by the answers you come up with.

Moving near your center once can be a difficult but rewarding experience. Staying there requires less work, but is no less important. If you value the clarity, peace of mind, and purpose that come with living at your center, make sure to do what you can to ensure you can stay as close as possible.

Your Center Is Always Moving

> **Never forget that your center is a moving target, not a one-time destination.**

Not only does life like to throw us curve balls, but each of us has a personality, priorities, and life circumstances that are always shifting and evolving. Just as my center isn't necessarily the same as your center, what felt centered to me three years ago might not work now... or my sense of center now might not still hold true a few years in the future.

That isn't meant to be discouraging, but to offer one more reminder that we can never stop growing and finding the next steps and the direction forward.

The fact that the process of seeking center never ends can seem like bad news, because it means that our work is never really done. But when you think about things more deeply, you find that that's actually thrilling and liberating – there is always more for us to embrace, and new parts of our personality to discover.

Even though finding inner peace doesn't mean achieving some Zen-like state where we are untroubled by everything around us, there is contentment and fulfillment to be found at your center. And, if we can discover that without being "tuned out" to our lives, but rather savoring every moment and experience (good or bad), then we are so much the better for it. We shouldn't seek to run from every challenge or bit of discomfort, but to make ourselves strong enough to embrace and overcome it. As the old saying goes, it doesn't get easier, we just get better. The struggle might be hard, but that's what makes us grow, and what makes the process of seeking center so fulfilling.

Chances are, you picked up this book because you realized you want something more from life. You're looking to discover a part of yourself that has remained hidden, or to feel a kind of contentment and direction that's been lacking, perhaps even despite personal and professional success. If you're willing to do the work needed to seek your center, I promise you can find it. Once you do, you'll start to wonder how you ever lived without the purpose and direction you have discovered, and you'll begin to see what kind of difference it can make in your career, your relationships, and the peace you can find within yourself.

I encourage you to come back to these chapters again in the future. In fact, you might want to read through this book a couple times a year to keep the core concepts, obstacles, and tenets of center alive in your consciousness. If you truly want to live near your center on a continual basis, it's important to keep in touch with yourself through the exercises and ideas we've already discussed. Remember that your center moves, and it takes a little bit of work to keep up with it.

All of us were born to seek center, and to live meaningful, engaged lives. If this book has helped you on that journey, then I feel like I have done my job and the difficult task of putting these words on the pages and screens has been well worth it. Once that happens, I would love to hear from you with your stories of success.

In the meantime, though, know that this involves a lifelong journey that's both easier and more difficult than it seems from the outside. I wish you success on that journey while you are *Seeking Your Center*.

Appendix 1

Searching for Center

*V*ery early in this book, I advised you to start a journal you can use to capture your thoughts on what your centered life might look like, how you can reach it, and what obstacles might be holding you back. If you've already started doing that, then you can use this section as a review and a way to see the "big picture" with all the key questions put together.

If you haven't started journaling, then I hope you'll take this chance to do it *right now*. The most important words in *Seeking Your Center* aren't the ones I've written, but the ones you add to my thoughts in your own notebook. This is the most important part of the process, since it requires your direct input. It's where the rubber meets the road. If you skip over the journaling, you're going to be back to a point where finding your center occurs randomly.

If you have put off journaling because it conjures up images of late nights in bed writing entries that begin with "Dear diary," then know from the outset I have a different kind of journaling in mind. Rather than simply scribbling down whatever might be on your mind at the moment, I'm going to ask you to do the complete opposite and ignore day-to-day ideas and distractions. I want you to tune out the "noise" and try to find which parts of your life are currently pulling you toward your center, and which ones are dragging you away.

Remember that there isn't a perfect time, method, or technique for answering the questions that matter most to you. Some people like to write in complete thoughts and sentences, while others will sketch out bullet points, or possibly even drawings. Any technique is fine so long as it works for you and helps to identify the parts of your life that are really working for you, as well as the ones that might need a bit more of your attention. Go on for page after page if it helps; stop and start, and then come back again; scratch out previous answers or add to them with new inspirations – any of these will work, and all of them will help you to move back toward your own center.

The only thing you absolutely shouldn't do is stop before you're finished. Whether it takes two hours, two days, or twenty weeks, keep coming back to your notebook when you have a few free moments. The goal here is to identify incredibly important factors that will lead you toward your center. My desire is to move you toward a level of conscious awareness that will increase the likelihood you can identify and experience a more fulfilling life. It's hard work. Don't look for shortcuts and you won't be disappointed with the answers.

Questions to Help Guide You Toward Your Center

Consider the questions you find below as idea starters that have been helpful to others. They might not cover all of the issues that matter to you, and not every question will necessarily be relevant to your situation. Still, in the same way that journalists and public speakers use note cards to organize their thoughts and conduct interviews to get to concrete answers, these questions can help get your mind moving. Add and expound as needed, but take enough time with each one in your journal to be sure you actually have the answer that's right for you.

YOUR CENTER

- *When in the past have you felt completely centered?*

- *What ideas or activities have captivated you completely and stand out as being the most memorable in your mind?*

- *What does it take to feel your center?*

YOUR INNER CIRCLE

- *Which people are most important in your life?*

- *Can you think of three or four times in your life when your inner circle was especially supportive to you?*

- *Do you have people in your inner circle now who aren't as positive or supportive as they could be?*

FINANCIAL HARMONY

- *How much money would be enough for you to feel satisfied?*

- *What would it take for you to enjoy more financial harmony?*

- *How could you use some of your financial resources to bring more happiness to your life and the lives of others?*

VALUES AND PRIORITIES

- *Which parts of your life are most in or out of alignment with your values?*

- *Do you have any personal values that are in conflict with one another?*

- *Are there any major changes you need to make to live in a way that's consistent with your personal values?*

SPIRITUAL AWARENESS

- *Is your spiritual belief system giving you strength and perspective when you need it most?*

- *How much attention do you pay to the spiritual side of your life?*

- *Are you letting the term "religion" distract you from a connection to your sense of spirituality? If so, what can you do to change it?*

YOUR PURPOSE

- *Do you feel like the life you live is a good match for your skills, talents, and desires?*

- *Does success in your chosen field (or your most prominent personal activities) make you feel proud and fulfilled?*

- *If you are at or nearing retirement, how can you repurpose your life for the next phase of your life?*

BALANCE

- *Can you identify any particular tenets of center that stand out the most in your mind for being fulfilled or unfulfilled?*

- *Do you have something that's going very well in your life or something that you feel is missing from your life?*

- *Which tenets of center are you spending most of your time and energy on?*

RESOURCES

- *Who in your life is living at or near their center?*

- *What qualities do they have that you would like to make your own?*

- *What is it about their life that makes it most obvious that they're at their center?*

OBSTACLES TO YOUR CENTER

- *What do you think are your biggest obstacles to reaching your center right now?*

- *How is your own skepticism preventing you from finding inner peace?*

- *What emotional baggage are you clinging to that is preventing you from reaching center?*

Finding the Answers That Pull You Toward Center

As I mentioned, most people will take a significant amount of time finding out what their centers look like. Often, the insight that we are looking for is hidden between layer after layer of old habits, thought patterns, and preconceived notions that aren't as powerful or beneficial as we give them credit for.

By simply taking the time to journal out our thoughts, though – using these questions as a starting point – things will typically begin to come into focus pretty quickly. What you may find, for example, is that you aren't truly living in a way that aligns with all of your values, that you place too much priority on money and not enough on your most important relationships, or that you have settled for a career path that doesn't match up to your true purpose and talents.

Each of these situations is as common as it is understandable. But by facing up to facts, instead of hiding from them or burying them deep inside ourselves, we can learn what our own centers really look like… and then take steps to move toward it.

Don't be discouraged if it seems like the initial answers you write down aren't getting you anywhere. Instead, think on things a little more deeply, turn to some of the men and women you trust most in your life, and ask yourself more specific questions that build upon the ones I have presented here.

Eventually, you'll come to a breakthrough and discover what your centered life really looks like. After you know that, you're miles ahead of others who have never gone through this process, and that much closer to living a more relaxed, energizing, and engaged life.

APPENDIX 2

A Quick Overview of Seeking Your Center

Throughout this book I've added emphasis to a few statements and concepts I feel are absolutely essential to understanding and reaching your center. In this brief section, I'm going to read them once more.

These represent just some of the most prominent pieces of the system for happiness and contentment that I've outlined up to this point. In that way, they make the perfect tool for a quick review – a way for you to remind yourself of what you need to reach your center on a daily or weekly basis.

However, they aren't a good substitute for reading the book and going through the exercises yourself. With that in mind, I encourage you to go through the process again, complete with a fresh journal, on a regular basis or whenever you feel like you've moved far from your center.

Living near your center is a wonderful thing, but it's also like trying to hit a constantly moving target. Your dreams, values, and priorities might not be the same today as they were last year, or the way they will be a year from now. Likewise, resources are going to come and go from your life, and you may find yourself stronger in one tenet than another.

So, take my advice and do as I do. Use these reminders as a way to keep yourself close to center throughout your day-to-day life, and never let the process of self-evaluation stop.

Seeking Center Recap

Finding your center is about that mental and spiritual place where there isn't any fear or doubt, no worries or regrets, just the simple joy of doing whatever you're doing. It's not just having a sense of inner peace; it's *having the acknowledgment and awareness* that you do, and knowing that you can come back to that feeling again and again.

Finding center – whether it's for a moment or a lifetime – usually involves *exhilaration, purpose,* and *fulfillment*.

Unless you are willing to examine your own ideas, beliefs, and motivations, nothing I can write is going to be of value.

People who are at or near their center exude a calm and confidence that seems impossible to those who don't have it.

Rarely do people find complete professional fulfillment when their personal lives are in tatters, or vice versa.

As long as you're breathing, it's never too late to start moving toward your center.

Your center isn't a stationary target, but a state of being that's always moving.

You definitely don't want to be the kind of person that will fall for anything. Neither, though, do you want to be the sort of person who won't *believe* in anything, either.

Spirituality is accepting that there is something bigger to the universe, and faith is putting a little bit of our trust into that something.

With faith, humans can cure diseases, find the strength to fight against tyranny, and walk on the moon... without it, the smallest setback will leave you filled with the kind of self-doubt that stops you from accomplishing anything at all.

Real peace of mind comes from knowledge and insight. Not caring isn't the same thing. One comes from faith; the other arises from being numbed to the world or ignorant of what's going on around you.

With those relationships, others in your life are constantly pulling you toward center; without them, the search for meaningful connections will always pull you away from your center.

Earning more money seems like an easy way to permanently improve our lives, but that viewpoint rarely turns out to be valid.

It should be obvious that living in alignment with our values is critical to finding center, if only because we see so many people who aren't doing either.

Without accepting some form of faith in a higher power, religious or not, you don't have an anchor to hold you near your center, especially when things get tough.

Finding your purpose is about self-discovery, not self-invention. In other words, you figure out where your talents and aspirations already lie, not try to create them on your own. You don't try to be something you're not, no matter how green the grass seems on some other side (or in some other personality or career path).

You should remain conscious of these five cornerstones of a happy, fulfilled life. All of them matter, and balance is the key.

There can sometimes be an enormous difference between those who are *centered* and those who are *professionally successful*.

Having the ability to motivate yourself toward a particular goal, especially when it isn't easy, is required for virtually any kind of success… and men and women who live near their center are by definition almost always successful.

If you make perseverance a priority, and exercise your faith in yourself and your values often enough, you'll discover that there really isn't anything that can hold you back.

We admire people who have loyalty and integrity because they represent something we should all aspire to in terms of personal strength. And, consciously or not, they show us how to use our actions and principles to move closer to center every day.

Acting charitably gives us more gratitude and increases our self-esteem. Both of these are great qualities for any person to have, and obviously allow us to feel more centered.

Humility is much more than acting in a humble way, though, or letting your confidence come through. It's actually about recognizing that we are all in this together, and that the human condition is universal.

The true basis of kindness shouldn't be that you want or expect someone to be kind to you in return. Instead, it's the recognition that, no matter what mood you're in or what you have going on in your life, others have the same issues and challenges to deal with, as well.

When your last breath comes, it isn't going to matter what anyone else thought about the way you should have lived your life, only whether you feel satisfied with it or not.

Some people would rather stay busy than confront the gaping hole they feel when they stop to think.

When you fail to search for your center, you leave things entirely to chance. If you don't search, you can't find.

If you surround yourself with people who are supportive – and who are trying to stay motivated and live lives that are in line with their own values – it's going to feel natural for you to do the same. And, if you're surrounded by others who are constantly negative, or make you feel worse about yourself, then you can't be surprised when those impressions rub off on you, either.

Stress and fatigue dull us to things that are going on around us, not to mention things that are happening *within* us. Being tired and stressed out affects the way you think about everything else in your life, making every day seem less sharp and less interesting – which is essentially the opposite of feeling centered.

The problem with negative emotions is that they are antithetical to our values.

No one escapes life unscathed, and we all know that carrying "baggage" is just part of life on Earth.

Unresolved expectations *always* lead to conflict.

Your comforter can also be a tremendous source of love and support. No matter how strong we are in our careers, or what we've accomplished in our personal lives, we all need someone who is "in our corner" from time to time.

Counselors are important to you in your life because they have unique training and experience they can use to show you ideas, patterns, and even inspirations that might be difficult for you to express consciously or openly.

Your spiritual advisor is an important resource – a "rock" who can keep you grounded in your faith, whatever that faith looks like.

A great mentor uses their wisdom and experience to help you become a better version of yourself, which is almost always a good step to take if you want to reach your center and make the most of your life.

A big effect in your life doesn't necessarily have to come from a big change.

Until you know exactly what you're looking for, you're always going to have a hard time finding it.

If you want to feel centered and fulfilled, you're going to have to make more room for things in some new parts of your life to grow. Once you've decided on a certain direction, commit to it and move forward without looking back.

Finding your center is something you have to *do*, and not something you can simply read about and *have happen to you*.

Finding your center isn't only about having experiences that are exhilarating and pulse-quickening. It's more about living every day to the fullest and feeling like you're slowly becoming the person that you were born to be.

Looking for your center automatically pulls you closer to it, raising your awareness of your dreams and intentions one step at a time.

We have to be aware that our center exists, and have the desire to keep moving toward it, no matter how hard life pushes in the other direction.

Never forget that your center is a moving target, not a one-time destination.

About the Author

Aside from being the author of *Seeking Your Center*, Tim Crain is a keynote speaker, financial executive, Certified Financial Planner, and U.S. Army veteran. Throughout his life and career, he has been interested in the concept of success and happiness, and particularly why so many people fail to find contentment within the "more and bigger" mindset found all over the world.

In his personal life, Tim has been married for more than two decades and has three fantastic children. He enjoys a number of active hobbies including aviation, scuba diving, boating, fishing, and other outdoor activities.

Seeking Your Center is Tim's first book. You can find more information about him, supplements to the book, and his speaking calendar at: www.SeekingYourCenter.com.

www.ingramcontent.com/pod-product-compliance
Lightning Source LLC
Chambersburg PA
CBHW032035290426
44110CB00012B/816